The Truth of All that Is

THE ANGEL BOOK

By

Amelia Bert

ameliabert.com

Copyright © 2016 by Amelia Bert

No part of this book may be reproduced in any form or by any electronic or mechanical means including information storage and retrieval systems, without permission in writing from the author. The only exception is by a reviewer, who may quote short excerpts in a review. For information address: http://ameliabert.com/

The methods describe within this Book are not intended to be a definitive set of instructions for this project. You may discover there are other methods and materials to accomplish the same end result.

This book is not intended to be a substitute for the medical advice of a licensed physician. The reader should consult with their doctor in any matters relating to his/her health.

For information on special discounts for bulk purchases, please contact via email at: amelia@ameliabert.com

Visit website at: ameliabert.com

First Printing: March 2016

CAUTION:

The contains of this book provide powerful information that will lead to spiritual growth and transformation. You are advised not to proceed if you hold negative intentions, fear and/or uncertainty, as the information provided will not be of benefit.

The information given are for the advantage of those who are ready for its content. This book is not intended to provoke nor offend.

TABLE OF CONTENTS:

Preface by the Angels ix
Preface by the Author xi
Introduction 1

PART I:
ENGLIGHTENMENT

1: Who you are, versus love and fear 5
2: Fifth dimension 11
3: Reincarnation 15
4: Who we are: Angels 19
5: Who is God? 23
6: Your power 27
7: You create your own world 29
8: The mind versus the heart 33
9: Spirit guides and life's purpose 37
10: Embrace all that you are 39

11: Who is this higher self? 43
12: Angel communication & signs 45
13: Blessings in disguise 51
14: Chakras 53
15: Express your true nature 57
16: Relationships 61
17: Children and their potential 65
18: Moving through Time and Space 69
19: Light and Darkness 73
20: Galaxy 77
21: Different dimensions 81
22: Circle of life 83
23: Afterlife 87
24: Prophecy 89

PART II:
CREATION

25: The world is your oyster 95
26: How the universe really works 97
27: Wish away 101
28: Three steps for materializing desires 105
29: Your desires await 109
30: The difference of needing and wanting 111
31: The power of focuses attention 115
32: The universe has a plan 117
33: Life review 121

34: When to Act 125
35: A letter for the future 127

PART III:
RELEASE

36: Welcome your new life experience 133
37: How to focus on your desires 137
38: Remove blockages 139
39: Deny limiting beliefs 143
40: Fear is an illusion 145
41: Learn to float 147
42: Levels of energy 151
43: Emotional responses 155
44: A manifestation technique 159
45: Achieve an abundant mindset 163
46: Go with the flow 167
47: Prepare for arrival 169

PART IV:
EMPOWEREMENT

48: Ask for a sign 173
49: The significance of your thoughts 175
50: Your everyday interactions 179
51: Divine opportunities 183
52: Allow Divine Energy within 187
53: Clear your thoughts and be happy now 189
54: Return to purity 193

55: Rewrite or delete	197
56: Everyday techniques	201
57: Shield yourself	205
58: Crown chakra	209
59: Connecting with your Higher Self	211
60: Mental powers of communication	215
61: Remember your talents	219
62: Fulfilling your life's purpose	223
63: You know the answer	225
64: Nature's blessings	229
65: We carry the pain away	231
66: Be a leader	233
67: Find your truth	237
68: Discover your potential	241
69: Signs of an awakened spirit	243
70: Your awakening	247
71: Message from God	249

PREFACE BY ANGELS

We write this book, to let you know of all you can achieve in this life, and in others. We enjoy moving you forward, watching you grow and expand. This book is to awaken you to your spiritual power. We guide you to reach your full potential, uncover your powers, reach your divinity and receive divine communication. If you are wondering whether all that is possible, we assure you that it is, since they are part of your nature. Read through the words of this book carefully, and learn to reawaken to the glory of who you are.

You have a lot of potential and you are never alone, we always look after you, guide you and restore you. But, you must want to change, to expand, to become better, to reach your spiritual power. Do not be afraid of this power, of what you will experience; let it move you so you can benefit the most. Our words bring power, but only for those who believe in them. We restore you to your divinity. All we ask, is that you allow us to guide you, do not deny our words, do not deny your power but follow your heart, your instinct, your will to become the powerful being that you came here to be.

We know the truth in this book contradicts many people's

views and beliefs on several matters. This is not a book to please all; only those ready for the change. If one reads with a mind full of doubt, disbelief or anger, one will not receive our Divine assistance through it. Jesus is not accepted by all, and that is alright; everyone is free to choose what they please. In another life, in another time, those who do not believe will be born again and change those beliefs, until they find the truth. For this, we will only point this book to those who are ready, who can change the world, and make way for others to follow. You have come a long way to hear us say those words to you, and if you accept them and read with an open heart, you will know them.

Nobody is forced to do anything, nor believe what we present. You picked up this book, because you are ready to find the truth of who you are, to reach your Divinity, to find your power, to reach divine communication. You are half way there; the road is easy after that. Leave judgment and fear and you will be on your way. This book is not to preach about your power, but to guide you to find it within. Allow us to move you to higher levels of expansion where your spirit lies.

Whenever you are ready, begin reading along. If you hold disbelief, denial and/or fear, you will not benefit, come again when you are ready. Let us to show you the way; we are present with you, ask us to protect you, help you acknowledge the truth.

This is the beginning of the rise for humanity. Free your mind, understand the ways of the universe, and be directed to all you are, and all you are created to be. The time is now to bring the change that most desire. The ascension began, the change is here, the love exists and conquers all.

The Angels

PREFACE BY AUTHOR

I welcome you to this journey of self-discovery. This is not an ordinary book, as the Angels narrated it to me. What you are about to read, is the truth, as it comes from Them, to benefit all of us. It answers questions many wonder about, as well as explores useful techniques that can help us discover our way and expand our spirit.

My name is Amelia. I was not born with the gift of mental communication; I crafted it, and so can you; we are all special in this way.

A few years ago, I came across the "Law of Attraction" and was fascinated by it. I studied it thoroughly, trying to find ways to change my life, and answers that would resonate with my spirit. I was also drawn to meditation; I found it a useful tool to enhance my being. For several months, I dedicated more than thirty minutes, each day to meditation. It made me feel peaceful, at ease, powerful.

One day before my meditation routine, I wanted to connect with my "Higher Self". I haven't done it before but I was curious. I knew there was a higher power in all, and I felt ready to experience it.

Not long after, while in meditation, a strong thought dominated my stillness.

"*We are here connecting with you now, do not be afraid. All is well.*"

I was not afraid; I was confused, because this "voice" was just a thought, with a striking resemblance to my own. I thought I imagined it, but I could not have, since I was in meditation and released from thought.

I asked; "*Who are you?*"
It responded;

"*We are the energy that flows through you and for you. We are the alignment of your desires; we are the answer to your inquiry. You asked us here and we responded. You are leading the way and we follow. We understand your journey and we help you achieve it. We are your guidance.*"

I spent hours writing down the answers that flowed through this inner guidance, my higher self. I wrote a question and the response came immediately through my own thoughts. I was excited and thrilled with the answers that flowed through me. They were always loving and made so much sense; I knew them to be true. In time, I crafted the skill of mental communication that I can now not only "hear" the thoughts given to me, but I can also "see" mental images, and experience emotions coming from my spiritual connection.

And like this, my spiritual awakening began. I understood, I made peace with myself and the world, I found my Divine Purpose; I expanded.

A month after this beautiful incident, I requested to communicate with the Angels. I chose the first Archangel that came to mind. Archangel Michael.

"*We are connecting in joy*", Archangel Michael spoke through me. This simple sentence resulted in a waterfall of emotional tears.

I didn't know it then, but it was just the beginning.

It's been several months since I began, and now I interact with different Angels, Ascended Masters, and Spirit Guides, and all of them respond; always. I feel peace, love and serenity. Their Divine Energies surround me, and connect through my thoughts and emotions. And so, my journey and lessons began. This book came to life to help you learn and expand from their guidance as well.

The Angels warned me of a great change but never explained what or how. They rarely tell you how things will occur, even though they see it, they know it can change and so they only reveal something once it is time.

It was 27th of May 2015, and Mother Mary connected with me through meditation. The thoughts that formed in my mind were so peaceful and accompanied by powerful loving emotions. The final words she spoke were: *"The time is now."*

On the same day, my ears began buzzing. It was the first time it happened in that way, but I knew the Angels tried to get my attention.

So I asked, *"Do you have a message for me?"*

The immediate response was: *"We want you to write a book with us. It is time now."*

I neither doubted their wisdom nor hesitated. I began typing on the computer and the words flowed in a clear and effortless manner. I wrote the introduction without any effort, and I was amazed at how well it turned out, and how everything made sense.

I never knew what each chapter would be about until it flowed through my fingers. Half of the things I wrote I already knew, others I learned for the first time, yet they all made sense.

Some chapters have different tone of voice than others, and

the word selection differs; this is because different Angels narrated each chapter. Each of them, like you and I, have a different voice, a different way of communicating, so each chapter is unique. Some are loving and humorous, while others are sharp and to-the-point but all of them resonate with love, energy and power.

Before each chapter, the Angels motivated me to cleanse my energies. In this way, each chapter only holds pure, positive vibration, and the words bring positivity, inspiration, and uplifting energy. They also prompted me to bless each and every book before it reaches you, to heal and surround you with their love. If you read with an open heart, you will shift yourself.

The Angels explain that this book is easy to understand as they want all of you, to enjoy it, and receive all of their messages. They did not want to expose you to deep, confusing explanations, so the chapters are brief. For this reason, the vocabulary is contemporary and simple to bring you clarity yet, every time you read it, you will gain something new.
As God says, *"I am not fond of many words."*

So, in this way, through the Angels and me, we present this book to you, to assist you in your own paths of discovery. I am so thankful to Them, and I hope this book is as life changing to you, as it was to me.

Please, proceed with an open heart
Amelia Bert

INTRODUCTION

The journey into co-creation began when you came into being, and formed endless possibilities and opportunities for yourself and others. The time has now come for you to ascend into higher realms of existence to experience more of the opportunities that you seek. This journey into co-creation, or the life in the physical world, should be effortless and unlimited.

People come and go everyday into the place you call "Earth", and while some achieve their life's purpose and ascend; others are once again taken upon the human journey of self-discovery to grow their spirit. When we say "ascend," we mean the journey of the soul once one completes their purpose, gains experiences, learns skills and achieves alignment with All-that-Is. Souls that gain all those traits, hold more Divine Power, like the Spirit Guides and Ascended Masters.

Those who read this book will find their spiritual path and purpose a lot easier than others. This book is here to assist you to grow, and ascend in mind and body.

In the world that you stand, there is a plethora of resources to grant you the fulfillment and joy you have been seeking, not only for material growth but also, for spiritual improvement. As you walk upon the paths you chose, you face troubles and joys. Most troubles come from your environment, that creates disbelief and disillusionment about values and right and wrong. For that, we are here to enlighten you and open your eyes to the truth of All-that-Is, to the spiritual awakening you need to expand.

The time you read this book, it is not a coincidence. You have been brought into this moment by your Spiritual Team that stays in the Divine and guides you every step along the way. This is the time to let go of old beliefs. Embrace the wholeness of who you are.

This book is a unique exception to all that has been done before, to assist all of you to spread your wings and follow us closer to love, closer to the Divine, closer to God – that Holy Power that lingers in each and every one of us, that is and always will be, a part of our being. You are unlimited, you are powerful, you are so loved and cared for.

> We are always here for you.
> Your Angels, Ascended Masters,
> Spirit Guides and God.

PART I:
ENGLIGHTENMENT

CHAPTER 1

WHO YOU ARE VERSUS LOVE AND FEAR

The knowledge that lies within this book will assist you in finding the truth of your creation and of the cosmic energy of All-that-Is. When you know, you become "awakened" by the information you have blocked out as you embarked upon this physical journey and like this, you can easily find your path and happiness. It is time to figure out the truth that lies within, of who you are, and of your purpose.

Humans embarked upon the journey of creation after they responded to the will of God, who instructed that energy should radiate in all forms, in all layers of existence. By doing so, all energy—souls, would benefit from their journeys. They will assist one another in creation, co-exist, and enjoy the blessings that each lifetime and dimension offers. And so, all of you were spread in existence into various layers or dimensions, each one taking different paths and assignments to fulfill, but all having the same goal: Enjoy each lifetime, learn, love and expand. And so it is.

Some of you moved into the physical dimension that is now where you reside.

There is Us, the Angelic Realm, that is closer to God, we speak His truth and are here under His direction, to assist all of you find your way.

There are also the Ascended Masters and Spirit Guides that once moved in human form, but now they have expanded; they have fulfilled their life's purpose and remain closer to us, to assist you expand as well.

There are the fairies and all those forms that exist, but are hidden from humanity. They subsist in different layers that the human eye cannot reach. They are also assigned roles that would serve many, Mother Nature and the cosmic expansion.

Also, there are various other souls - civilizations beyond human eye that co-exist fully among each other, and are more evolved than three dimensional beings like yourselves. They are closer to the Divine, and their power is more recognized, but they too, have expansion to undergo. They all exist to serve their life's purpose and the will of God, co-existing in various forms and different layers or dimensions that we explain in later chapters.

We are all beings of God, and we are holy; we have His blessings and powers. We are all different, yet so alike. We all co-exist to fulfill our paths and expand. You, our dearest brothers and sisters, are here to evolve, to live, to enjoy the beauty, to radiate good, and to embark into the next stage of your glorious lifetime.

Indeed, you live never-endingly, always evolving, always learning, and coming closer to your path and Divine Purpose.

There is so much glory, beauty, and Divine Energy to who you are, and we will tell you again, and again, until you discover it also. We believe in your power. Embark upon this journey of awakening and let yourself be moved by the beauty that is all around. Let yourself expand and radiate Divine Energy, believe that you came here for something bigger.

Each of your lifetimes is blessed and Divinely chosen by you before you embarked upon this journey. All of you serve a different Divine Purpose in each duration of life, and it is time to find what that is and fulfill it. As you do, you will be reborn more Divine, more purified, more powerful, closer to God. Each lifetime brings you wisdom, knowledge and helps you expand and shift in the direction that you choose. There is one path; however, that you physical beings share the same: Live with the pure positive emotions that love brings.

God lives through all of us and enjoys the pleasures as much as you; God loves to watch you learn, expand and enjoy your life. But something happened along the way that blocked you from having more of the positive experiences. You are controlled by fear, and that limits your ability to love and live a beautiful abundant life. But what has happened? Why have you become so?

We do not blame you, for we know you came to experience all. But you give emphasis on the things that are not pleasing, and so you invite them in your life. You deserve good experiences, and you can get them. The question is, do you want them, and are you ready to receive them? Are you willing to step away from what is not serving you to have All-that-Is, all that you came here to be? We knew the reply, and so we have guided you towards this book that is the answer to what have you wondered. You have asked us here, consciously or not, and we respond to your plea for assistance. You, who read now, have wondered what you can do to have a better life. Whatever you need to know is in this book; read it carefully and if you struggle, ask us for help. We are here.

The question remains, what has brought you to this? Very early in the beginning of your creation, you were all happy and enjoyed existence. You lived by the will of God and were pure and Divine, with no blockages or limitations. You could talk to us and God directly and we had long beautiful conversations. But for you to expand and grow, you had to live on the other side of ways. In order to appreciate love, you needed to come across fear. Fear is necessary to understand the importance of love. And as you choose love, you grow and live with joy, but you stayed in fear. It has blinded you; some of you found it too overwhelming and could not comprehend why God allowed you to experience that. You then called Him a vengeful God, and declared that your punishment. You convinced yourself that you are worthy of the fear and so you stayed in the shadows. Our loving brothers and sisters, fear was created only to see how blessed you are to have love. Your free-will should be the one of love and beauty, and not fear and unworthiness.

After this, you created religions that talk about punishment and you made up the Devil that would be responsible for the bad in your lives, as you cannot see that the bad are a blessings as well. You differentiated it from God in order to love God. But devil does not exist, only the retraction from love, that is all it is.

Love is any pure positive emotions that comes from the Light. And fear is any negative emotion. For one to exist, the other shall be also. If it weren't, you would not appreciate it as it is. You would not know its glory, nor what it means. Think of it like a rabbit that grows in a hole. All its life it is in that hole, living, eating, breathing experiencing only that which that place brings. That rabbit has no choices, it doesn't know there is life beyond that, and so it cannot appreciate the world, it cannot know the Light because it doesn't know it exists. When it digs and frees itself into the world, it knows the Light, it has choices, stay or go. The rabbit gains knowledge of the darkness and the Light, of the small hole and the big world. You see in this way, you need to experience all to understand what exists, make your choices, and learn.

You came for a cause and a path, but since all beings that walk on Earth undergo a time of limbo, all of the truths are blocked. This is so you live and enjoy human life, expand, make your own choices and learn from them. As you choose to be close to God and to your truth, live by love and appreciation; you will be guided to your life's path.

Some will say: *All this, is a test of God to test our will and devotion to Him.* We say: *All are necessary to learn lessons and expand.* There would be no lessons learned if you knew the Truth-of-All-that-Is when you incarnated in human form. This way, you are now filled with life teachings that make your soul wiser.

There is so much of the Divine Truth that cannot be said through the words of this book, worth lifetimes and centuries of information of who you are, and how we all came about, but we only grasp the basics to help you understand your potential.

And so, now you realize why the bad needs to exist to appreciate the good. By acknowledging the good you attract more of them into your experience. We are here to reawaken you into the beauty. We answer your pleas, we surround you with love and teachings; *and this book is our guidance.*

We will always be here to help you expand, bring you on your path, and lift your spirits. We are humble beings of existence taken upon the task to assist you, and for that, we are here now, doing so with so much love, devotion and appreciation of who you are and of what you came here to be

                                              You are all very special to us.

CHAPTER 2

SPIRITUAL AWAKENING AND FIFTH DIMENSION

In early years of creation, you resided in the fifth dimension, but due to fear and insecurity you moved to the third dimension you now live. In the third dimension, your purity, love, and happiness is overshadowed by fear and struggle. The days of darkness and fear are coming to an end; you are returning back to love; you are returning to the fifth dimension.

When we say "dimension" we do not mean a place, but a spiritual plane. Each plane has different advantages for the energy beings that reside within. We, the Angels, exist in the thirteenth (13th) plane, and you used to be in the fifth (5th). We could not prevent the "fall" from the fifth dimension, as we could not interfere with your free-will. By making your own choices you learn and gain experiences. God allows you to live as you choose, and the third dimension is only a place of learning. You do not need it any more; you have acknowledged how the world is; you saw fear and now you are to return to love.

The return to the fifth dimension is a blessed and beneficial change. It is not a physical change but a spiritual ascension. Your surroundings will stay intact, but you will change. Your power, views, interactions, and the way you see the world will shift for the better. You will embrace your spirit, and value the ego less. Fifth dimension is a state of living closer to the words of God and closer to your purified self. You will live more peacefully, with no struggle, or fear, and create your desires with ease. You will hold pure positive emotions; you will be awakened by your surroundings, and more connected to your neighbors.

The shift to the fifth dimension has already begun, and it occurs gradually. It is achieved once you "awaken" spiritually, release worries and struggles, once you realize your strengths, and become reawakened to your potential – this way you will spread love, appreciation and kindness. This is what you call "awakening" or "spiritual transformation." It is the purpose of this book; to help you naturally rise and find your way towards the fifth dimension. If we succeed in that, and whether you have indeed awakened, you will discover by the end of your read.

Not all are ready for this change and no-one will shift to the fifth dimension, unless they choose to, unless they allow their divinity to take the lead.

The old are about to be released, and new will take their place. Be ready to awaken into all that you are and all you can achieve. Once you do, you experience a radical change that moves you into the fifth dimension. This way, you transform your life experiences into joyful opportunities, as well as expand your spirit in power and energy. You gain a knowing of All-that-Is true and of all that serves you. If you use these new ideas, you shift purified, glorious and blissful.

You should not be afraid of this change, because it is one of release, expansion and freedom. This shift is needed to bring you closer to love and to all your potential. Once your senses awaken into these ideals, you will begin to expand and grow, be happier, and in control of your reality. Like this, you can create miracles. As you move spiritually in the fifth plane, you will be closer to us and communication will be easier as you will receive our messages freely and even consciously.

Your "awakening" benefits all of humanity, too. More people that hold purified energies means bigger release of old ideals and darkness. For this, the Angelic Realm and your Spirit Guides, are in a mission to awaken more of you and restore humanity into its pure nature. Read, believe and return to the glorious days of existence when humans walked on Earth awakened by their truth, inspired by Divine Light and master of their world. You are now to return into these higher levels of state of mind with no struggle, no disappointment and no hate.

This shift, is a change that God instructed: physical beings to return to higher realms. *You are rising.* This is the end of the world as you know it, not because it shall cease from existence, but because it is to be replaced in perspective.

Embrace the changes that are coming to you. Follow your intuition, live in peace and happiness. Appreciate what you now have as they will be replaced with better ones. You are evolving. We are eager and expectant to see you uplift and grow spiritually, because you have miracles to create and experiences to enjoy. It is time for all of you to make the shift. We want to see you fly.

Are you ready?

CHAPTER 3

REINCARNATION

You are not a physical being that has a spirit, but a spirit that has a physical body. There is not an end to the journey of the soul. God created you to live, and not to die. There is not an end to the world you stand; it was created to be savored and not destroyed. In this chapter we explain a soul's journey so you do not fear an end.

The journey of your soul, always moves forward. When you are born in a body, you embrace it to enjoy all the experiences which that life brings. The body, however, becomes weak and fades with years, but not your soul. The soul never fades; it expands and gains knowledge, and then continues its journey without the body, because it has offered you all the expansion you need. When that is so, you join another journey, to gain more experiences, knowledge, and expansion. Change is blessed; if one lives in the same body for 1,000 years, they have nothing new to gain or give. The time one has on each physical body, is enough to complete their mission and gain experiences needed to grow.

After a soul releases its physical attachment, it moves to higher levels of existence, where it is happy, pure and free. It is not saddened by passing, nor does it have any blockages to keep it grounded. Once the soul separates from the body, it leaves memory and mind behind, but it keeps the teachings and wisdom.

On rare occasions, those souls that did not yet complete their life's path, or they have lived by the ego, they are blinded by negative emotions such as: fear, sadness, guilt. Those souls, then, do not allow themselves to be free and stay close to the physical plane, yet with no physical shield. Those souls you call them "ghosts". In those rare instances, those souls are still governed by their ego and hold many blockages that confuses them from returning to their divinity, and they stay close to the physical plane. Their guardian angels attend to assist them to continue their journey, but free will always is in charge of destiny. If they decide, they can easily find their way and continue their path.

We do not give you this information to frighten you, as those instances are few and those souls choose their own path. Once one detaches from their physical body, they are filled with unconditional love, appreciation, euphoria and are naturally guided by their Angel towards higher planes. Every soul then chooses their next journey so they live and expand some more, and the journey of the soul never ends.

There is not a physical plane such as Paradise or Heaven or Hell that many of you refer to; but there is a spiritual plane where all souls go to reemerge with their Higher Self and stay in love, peace and unity. As are not a physical being that has a spirit, but a spirit that has a physical being, when you let go of your physical vessel, you soul is abstract, like Light: untouchable, and yet so full and complete. Your non-physical self is a mass of positive vibrations, joyful emotions and love. You are Divine in nature, and you return to that state, again. There is no attachment, but there is free will. All souls choose their next journey, move as they please and reincarnate in the place of their choosing. You may come back to Earth, you may move in other planes, but your journey continues.

You shall not fear of an end, because that will never be. You always expand and continue to live free, regardless the body. Do not fear death, as that is but a beginning of a new experience. "Hell" does not exist; all that exists is a Heaven of emotions, completion and love. Enjoy each physical journey, learn, expand and empower your being with positivity and good experiences, until that body wears down, and your journey continues greater and wiser.

You are eternal.

CHAPTER 4

WHO WE ARE (ANGELS)

We have communicated with you directly and indirectly throughout several moments of your life. We always respond to your call and prayers; it is our work that God assigned for us, and we are more than happy to fulfill. In this chapter we inform you of our existence, and how we assist you.

We exist in higher dimensions, usually the thirteenth (13th), and even though it is several layers away from where you are, we can always travel with ease and reach you at the speed of Light. We move like energy flows. We do not have wings like many of you think, but we are a mass of energy and Light that travels at will. We do not have a material form, but we think and interact with anything that has energy. We have certain qualities and we use them with focused attention to lovingly assist anyone in need. They call us Angels by name, and we are beings that speak the word of

God. We are all created equally and hold no exceptions among us. We understand that all is energy and so everything is equal. God is another word for us, for we interact in the same manner and preach the same words. There is no difference among who we are and who you are. We are all God; yet, some of you are more connected to their divinity and to what you call Source or God, or All-that-Is. We are among those beings that do not hold ill intentions or suffered a "fall".

For each one of you physical beings, there are two Guardian Angels to watch over you, perhaps more. They bring you circumstances, people and events to assist you in your life, undergo a problem, heal over a wound, cover certain needs or even show you the way towards your desires.

We, the Angels, usually connect with you directly from within your mind, but most of you are too busy to hear us. If you clear your mind from troubles and thoughts, you will follow our assistance directly. There is no exception to this gift. All of you can connect with us in this way.

Amelia, our loving mediator, has achieved this beautiful interaction after months of devotion and focused attention in clearing her mind. She meditated for days, never missing one. When she asked us to appear, we did. We couldn't interfere with her free will otherwise. She was removed from clutter and was able to capture our words, even though they were so close to her own. In time and practice, she managed to differentiate the two and so here we are, talking to you through her.

We can be in many places at once, for we are energy that radiates, and we hold no sense of time or place. We may surround you in the Light or reside inside your mind and emotions, to bring you our guidance. Any time you focus your attention on us, we always move towards it. We protect you if you ask, show you the way, enrich you with our energies, and heal you from within. Have no fear, for as long as you hold your belief in us, nothing unwelcome can touch you, or befall you, for you are protected. You are an extension of us and we are an extension of you. We all have God residing inside, and for that we are always blessed.

We strengthen you in power; we watch over you and assist you even if you are not aware. Your power lies beyond what you see, and you have mighty support. You are our brothers and sisters by nature, as we are both created from the same focused thought. We are both spirit and all have expansion to undergo and paths to fulfill. Whether you believe in us or God, we do not care, for we only see the beauty of who you really are. You all receive Divine guidance, consciously or unconsciously every day. God makes no exceptions; you all are equal and special in our eyes.

All of you have exceptional power; you must believe in yourself and find it within. We assist you in every step. You are our brothers and sisters, you are like us.

We are here.

CHAPTER 5

WHO IS GOD?

What is the reason for this world in which you stand? How come we have been scattered in different places, different layers? What is the purpose of what you came here to be? You come from different experiences, different existences, yet you are all the same; you may even knew each other before, but today everything is new, unknown, undiscovered. Here, we bring you the reason behind everything, the knowledge of the missing puzzle; we bring you the truth of how it all began.

There is not one God, one entity, one being that conquers all and is the strongest of all of you and us. One such God does not exist; nor are you ancestors of Adam and Eve. There is no distinction between you, and of All-that-Is. It is not you and the "other" for there is no other; you are All-that-Is. There is not one source of power that controls all the others, but the same power exists in all. You are not different than us, for we are all a soul of Light, Divine Power and love. We are all interconnected, one completes the other; we are unity, creation, All-that-Is. God exists, but He is not a powerful, old being that is called your Creator. This powerful Energy exists, lives and breathes within each and every one of us. God is holy energy, God is Light, God is in all forms of life, God is you, and God is us.

You should not make a distinction among yourselves, for you are all Divine and parts of the same God. When it all began, God or Source Energy, was all that was; only one existed, alone. This Energy always been, but it extended to understand its existence, its abilities, its powers. Then this Energy began to formulate and expand and create. The more it created, the more it expanded, the more it learned the power that it had. This Energy then began to form thoughts, radiate energy, and create universes and alternative worlds. This Energy separated and moved to formulate, experience and live in as many forms as it could, so It can understand Its power and existence. And so, the cosmos was created, and the stars and the planets, and you and us. We are all parts of that Energy of God that now lives through us, and experiences, and lives, and learns, and expands. God sees all, knows all, is all and in this way, completes expansion, experiences, understands its creation.

And so, we are all one, parts of the same holy power that is pure and good and is All-that-Is. We are the stars and the planets and we can create miracles and we can sense each other and love each other, because all is an extension of us. God, though us, expands with every knowledge, every choice, every lifetime. You are never ending, you are holy and powerful as you are parts of that Energy. God made you, and made us, as a way to experience beauty and love. And so, here you are, on your way to your glorious awakening to come closer to your purity and understand your godly power.

We are here to help you rediscover your Source Energy, to find your Divine Self. Expect miracles, for you are a very powerful creator.

You are All-that-Is.

CHAPTER 6

YOUR POWER

All that exists, was first attention. Everything that surrounds you now, ideas, people, objects, animals or plants, even circumstances, are created from focused thought. And in this way, the world was created. In this chapter we explain just how powerful you really are.

God, who is Energy that always existed, gave focus on the planets and the stars and they began to form and appear. Then God gave attention in the surroundings, and the cosmos was created. The same way we, the Angels, came about and later human beings. We were all created by God's focused attention. From energy, we were given energy to formulate and some of this energy exists in all creations. We are parts of God.

The same way God's creates, you do as well; with your focused attention. Of course God is very powerful, and thus formulates anything from a slight focused attention; you, on the other hand, hold blockages and worry, and thus your power needs crafting. If you use the teachings we bring you into your everyday experience, these blockages will be removed leaving you more powerful and connected with your holy power. And then, you can create miracles.

Before we explain about this power further, we bring you a forewarning: *Use your power with only love in your heart and remember that all are creations of God as well.*

We give this forewarning because with that power, you create good things and bad. You have misused that power on several occasions before. You even create disasters and sicknesses just because you put your attention towards them. This is why Earth "has fallen" from more divine dimensions: Instead focusing in matters that serve many, attention is given to destruction that brings corruption and panic. You do create miracles, so use them for a good cause. Anything that you attend to, we advise you to do for the greatest and highest good of all. As you do, you gain more power and your divinity becomes greater. Destruction and corruption is not in the means of God and humanity is advised to serve love and harmony. Take back your power and use it for good. We bring you a powerful wake-up call and a reminder of all you have forgotten. We bring you the means to reawaken you, to take back your power, and form miracles. In doing so, you become more powerful, skilled, and you can truly bring miracles on Earth. Use the practices and means of this book for personal and universal expansion. You are an angel on Earth, and you were created by God to bring miracles. Do so.

God exists in all of us, be awaken to His glory, find your Divine Power. Keep reading, and you shall discover it in great detail. We believe that you are ready. It is the time to begin this journey alongside us.

Humanity needs you.

CHAPTER 7

YOU CREATE YOUR OWN WORLD

There are no limitations in the world in which you stand. You came to create alongside with others, to wonder, interact, play, love, discover and ascend. You are on Earth to gain new experiences and interactions, fulfill your heart's desires and complete your life's purpose. There is nothing in this world that you cannot do; as *you create your world*. You are indeed very powerful, but first you must understand this power.

We do not compliment you, for whatever we entail is true. There is a deeper power within you that needs to be realized in order to uplift and enjoy life, complete your spiritual path and grow. That is the power of focus and energy; with it, you can create miracles. There is nothing unattainable, nothing evil, and there is no failure, only lessons learned that grow and expand you. You are destined to succeed, and that is what we want you to do.

You create your world by focusing on a specific matter for several seconds. With the energy of your focus, you cause it to expand that is then captured by the cosmos. There, the energy matches with more circumstances, events or people and radiates more energy, to return back to you. Be aware, however, that the attention you give may bring you joyful interactions and results, but also unpleasant ones. All are relative to the vibration of the thought you emit with your attention. If you focus on unpleasant experiences and feelings, then more follow, if your attention is on positive experiences, then more follow. Be aware of what you give out constantly, as that impacts how pleasurable and fulfilled your life will be.

An irritable person speaks ill words and does not take a moment to see the beauty that surrounds them; he radiates dissatisfaction, and so his world is unpleasant. If he recognizes happy moments in all experiences and appreciates them regularly, then the cosmos will respond to his satisfaction and sent equivalent ones to please him.

Even we, beings in higher realms, live by this "law." However, we have set our tone to love, forgiveness, appreciation, and joy, so we only radiate those pure emotions and nothing else. Negativity and ill behaviors are an extension of the human mind, as it steps away of the realm of love and the Divine. Ergo, we try to awaken you to the pure intentions and glory the Divine brings, to return you to your natural state. For this, we ask you to follow your true impulses, and find love in every corner. Focus on the positive aspects, and see there are more than plenty in this world you stand in; if you notice blessings, then more blessings shall flow into your experience, expand you, and allow more positive experiences to occur easily and abundantly. We help you understand and apply this in later chapters. For now, take a moment and contemplate upon the positive aspects of your life and be grateful.

Say: *"Thank you for all those moments that I felt pure and happy; thank you for this moment right now that I am alive and radiate energy. I recognize that I create my own reality, and I am to use that for good, for myself and for all."*

As you recognize the happy experiences, you not only assist yourself, but also humanity by radiating positive energetic flow and uplifting energy into the world. In this way, you cause positive expansion to enter your life, as well as in others'. As you bring joyful, positive energy into the cosmos, the more of it radiates within the cosmos, and the more positive material and spiritual things will be available to many. As you assist yourself, you assist humanity.

As you grow, you learn; as you expand, you increase in power. This is true for this lifetime as well as in others. In each lifetime there are lessons learned, and you always gain something in spirit. Never underestimate the power that you hold, for it is all that you need to succeed. You are positive and pure by nature. You matter, you are worthy and glorious. You can create the world you want to have. May we together bring the world closer to love, closer to its Divinity.

We absolutely adore you.

CHAPTER 8

THE MIND VERSUS THE HEART

Inspiration comes from the heart and not from the mind. When the mind doubts the heart, it does not allow the soul to flourish. Most of the time, you follow your mind passively, but this is not the way that you were created. Usually, whenever the mind, or the ego self does not understand an information, it denies it. But why was this ego created? Angels and Spiritual Beings, do not have egos, but humans do, as it serves its own purpose, alas if overused, it overcomes the spirit.

Your mind is filled with thoughts; it helps you rationalize, create and experience in various ways. The mind gives you choices and allows you to embrace your physical body that grounds you with mother Earth. Your mind, also holds the ego self. Your ego contains any characteristics or differences that you have, to exclude you from the crowd: your color, ethnicity, preferences, talents, skills, character, memories, or anything that you experience in physical body, effects the ego. It brings you pride, individuality, uniqueness. Unfortunately, it also replaces the power of unity and your spirituality. Your ego's major flow is: it excludes you from anything else other than itself. Jealousy, hate, selfishness and greed come from the ego in an extreme attempt to show you your individuality. Your ego has excluded you from others, from your Higher Self and your divinity. You use your mind more than you heart, you follow your thoughts more than your instinct, and so you move further away from your spirit, from your soul and its divinity.

We love that you have different ideas and different characters; this is what makes you unique. If you were all the same then you will not experience anything different, but only make the same choices, choose the same path and never evolve. Your individuality matters to what you become, what you decide and what experiences you gain, but not to who you really are.

Once you return to spirit, you leave your ego behind, the differences no longer exist, you are one with all, you reemerge to wholeness and love; you do not need your mind nor your differences; you are whole alongside all others. You are created from one, you become one. To deny the ego, you flourish the spirit. The ego serves you and this is why it was created, but use it to embrace your now and not limit your whole; there are many gifts waiting to uncover as you allow the spirit to take over.

Your desires do not appear if your mind is in control. You over-think, stress and worry, sees others' happiness and strive to succeed, to be better, to have more. When your mind is in control, your ego denies anything other than itself; it excludes you, leaving you lonely. But none was created to be lonely; you always are the happiest when you are around those you love; you are whole in this way. When you over-use your ego, you are supplied with negative responses of hatred, jealousy, doubt and fear; you bring misery. In this book, we teach you to silence the ego and follow your heart. Your mind may say one thing but your heart another: what do you do then? Most of you follow rationality, but why do you think you are given a different response from the heart? The heart brings you validity, guidance and love, follow it and you will not be mistaken. Put your heart in control and it will take you into the most beautiful life experiences.

    This chapter is specifically for those who doubt this book. Do not read with your mind, read with your heart; your heart knows and guides you towards the truth; it evolves you in spirit. We understand that the information may be new, and different from what you know in this physical life, and so it is natural to ignore it, as most are fearful of the new, of the unknown. That is alright, we do not change you, and we do not want you to change, for we love you just the way you are, no matter your choices, but you have come upon these lines for a reason: to expand your spirit; for that to happen you must silence the ego. Go with your heart, and not the mind in control. If you do that, you will find the truth within.

    We still love you all the same.

CHAPTER 9

SPIRIT GUIDES LEAD YOU TOWARDS YOUR LIFE'S PURPOSE

Each and everyone of your lifetimes is chosen carefully by you, before you followed them, based on the experiences you wanted to live, the skills you wanted to acquire, and the assistance you could provide. You also chose your physical family, and even your spiritual team such as Spirit Guides, that assist you since birth. Nothing is random, nor the place you reincarnated into, nor the people, the lessons, nor the life's path. Your Spirit Guides make sure you do not lose your path.

Spirit Guides follow you through several lifetimes. Perhaps they were a friend or a lover from another time on earth, or even a lovely pet that has passed on. Each and every one of your Spirit Guides knows you and loves you. They have chosen to follow and assist you to succeed your goals and life path. They send you guidance and signs to show you the right path. They know what you want, what is your path, and they assist you towards it. Their signs can be anything from a song that plays on the radio, or words of another person. Assistance comes in a variety of ways and we will direct you towards them, as you read along.

Your Spirit Guides, lead you towards your Divine Purpose. Become more aware, more alert of what is happening around you, because your purpose is waiting to be revealed.

You embarked upon this journey to create, offer to humanity, and fulfill your path in order to ascend. This life purpose can be an invention that progresses technology or a profession that heals or teaches others to be better. It brings healing, love, appreciation and happiness. It serves the masses, makes the world a better place and brings you expansion. Whatever this life's path may be, it is valuable.

Ask your Spirit Guides to reveal your life's path and notice what appears in patterns. Be ready to receive. You are never alone in this journey, and you knew that when you chose to reincarnate into this world. You have made your choices and then instructed your Spirit Guides and Guardian Angels to look out for you, guide you. And so, they all have. They have pointed you towards this book also. They want you to awaken and see the glory of this world, find your divinity, live in love and complete your Divine Purpose. There is Divine help everywhere you turn and there is no random circumstance on the road you have taken. Be alert and notice the world all around. We are talking to you.

Hear us.

CHAPTER 10

EMBRACE ALL THAT YOU ARE

Each being then was assigned a task to fulfill, a Divine plan, a purpose. You have been assigned a role for each lifetime, and your life guides you to it. In this world in which you stand, you exist because you have not yet completed your mission. Now, we guide you to find it.

Your Divine mission brings you reassurance, happiness and bliss. It is a path you want to follow eagerly and with anticipation. It fulfills you, pleases and excites you. This purpose entails all the gifts you hold in your being. All you have to do, is unravel those gifts and you will be guided to your Divine mission. Notice your gifts, recognize them, and accept them.

What are your preferences? What do you love doing, what completes you? If you didn't have any blockages in your way, what would you want to achieve? Make a list with all your talents, preferences and gifts. Perhaps you are gifted to assist others find their path, preach them values and lighten their way; or perhaps you prefer a road of peace and contemplation. Nothing is random; put the pieces together and you are going to be leaded to your path.

All your gifts and characteristics matter in any direction you wish to take. No one is happy doing what they dislike. Someone wants you to become a doctor, or a lawyer, but why please them and bring yourself misery? Do not lie to yourself, do not deny your gifts for they will lead you to your purpose, they will bring you joy and completion.

Your talents, characteristics, skills are important since you have crafted them diligently through various other lives to serve you unconditionally, so use them with pride and ease. Those gifts are there to help you fulfill your Divine Purpose. Do not hide in the shadows or behind others' preferences. It is wise to contemplate and discover yourself, rather than spent a lifetime hiding in another's path.

So what if you are older in years? That is not an excuse to live in misery; you exist because you have a task still. There is always time to find it and fulfill it. Make no excuses, do not withhold your talents, do not hide from who you are. Uncover your truth, find your gifts and preferences, use your talents. Why do you think each one has different predilections? All are different and all have paths to follow and missions to complete. Your preferences hide your individuality, your gift, your path.

Perhaps you are coy and proud in character; do not hide it. You are who you are and you have your suitable path. Embrace all that you are, love yourself. You are special in any way you are created, in any form you live, in any thought you have and in any mission you have to follow. Some may not like it, but you should. You are exceptional, and you hide many gifts; discover them, use them. Find your path; we lead you to do it.

You are guided.

CHAPTER 11

WHO IS THIS HIGHER SELF?

Higher Self, higher consciousness, higher mind or inner self are all the same, an extension of you in the non-physical. This part of yourself, exists in higher dimensions and is constantly with you. It is time to get acquainted.

You are material as well as spiritual. You have been created as one soul, a spirit, a ball of energy, like us, and your task is to expand and grow and learn and live in joy. But to do that, a part of you should exist in the non-physical to show you the way and keep you connected with your divinity. It is a way to remain pure forever. As you reincarnate on Earth, the bigger part of you still resides in the non-physical and when you die, you re-emerged again and become whole once more.

This part of you, or your Higher Self, or inner being, is truly pure and Divine, and holds a lot of potential and skills by all your other lifetimes. The more you connect, the more skilled you become, you remember truths, you feel whole, Divine, joyful and live life in a higher dimension. Think of it like two people who begin to know each other. At first they are strangers but then they learn details about one another, they bond and benefit from their interaction, pass on knowledge, skills, wisdom and joy. The more two people are connected, the more they benefit especially if one is truly wise and skilled. Your Higher Self has too many things to teach you, wisdom to share; it knows your boundaries, what you came here to achieve and guides you towards their completion. In fact, you are part of this self that came here, on this physical journey. It is an extension of you.

As you match thoughts and ideas that make sense to you, you are a match to your Higher Self. The more aligned you are with your true nature, the more powerful you become.

The practices we refer to in this book reconnect you back to this Higher Self. There are a lot of benefits when you do. If you pay attention to your thoughts and clear the chatter in your mind, then it becomes easy to receive this inner wisdom. It is a voice inside your head, a thought similar to yours, as they are you.

Listen to yourself, trust your intuition, your feelings, you are not alone, your Higher Self is taking care of you. You have inner wisdom and power already within. Sense and feel your holy connection. You are truly blessed and wonderful, you are Divine, and pure and powerful,

If you could find out how.

CHAPTER 12

ANGEL COMMUNICATION & SIGNS

You refer to us as Angels. We do not have a physical form, but we are only energy. We are here to assist you. We connect with you throughout various instances in several times in your life: We guide you forward, assist you to release negativity, uplift you. We do not want to cause you fear, and for this, our responses are always loving, reassuring and calm. We respect your free will and never affect your choices. Below we describe how we connect with you, so you can receive our messages directly.

How would you feel if you saw a mass of energy laying above you? You will surely be threatened and block any assistance coming from that energy. For that, we never appear in that way. You do not see us as the ball of Light that we are; but sense the calm and beautiful emotions of unconditional love, knowing and reassurance that we bring. We often shower you with these feelings to uplift and reassure you everything will turn out in your favor. The strongest emotion that you can have is the one of unconditional love. Usually this emotion is positive and it elevates you in all parts and in all ways. In that moment you love everything, anyone, you love where you are, all that you are; you become complete. Usually, you will sense the emotional power, and cry the warmest tears. Take more deep breaths and be in the moment more frequently, to expand your energies into the feeling of unconditional love. That is how God loves you.

We connect with changes in the atmosphere such as: the drop of a temperature in a certain spot near or above you. Also, we usually bring clean air in your lungs. When that occurs it may feels like the breath you took when near a lake, or the sea. If you notice such an air indoors, it is us cleansing the air that you breathe and make our presence known.

Chills or warm sensations, or even the feeling of water dropping on your skin - it is our touch on your physical skin. Flashes of Light, shiny coins, sun beam or anything that brings Light in, are signs from us, also. Feathers are common because we know you associate us with wings. Numbers that repeat over and over try to get your attention to bring you a message. An event, advice, object, website or anything that keeps repeating it is for you to acknowledge and act upon it. For instance, have you been seeing this book repeatedly before you finally decided to read it? Or perhaps something kept reminding you of it? Anything as that can be, know that we, or any Divine Being that assist you, want you to move forth, so we bring you patterns to get your attention. Be more aware of recurrent events; they are never coincidences.

The ways or messages we choose, vary, and are truly unlimited. Some of us choose different techniques to pass on a message either direct or indirect. All ways, however, are associated with intuition, your known gut reaction, a feeling that something is true, even if you cannot explain it. Reassurance from us is stronger, while sometimes sudden and fast; this is so due to your resistance of our energies, out of fear or doubt. We guide you through your subconscious.

Your intuition brings you warnings and guidance from your subconscious. In this way, everyone has a deeper knowing on how the world works, the truth that surrounds them, and even what needs to be done at a specific time to get certain results. Your subconscious is linked with your inner guidance or else your Higher Self that communicates to you through your emotions. A tightening in your stomach known as "a gut feeling" for instance, is the response of your subconscious to alert you of something negative. Perhaps you see someone new for the first time, but you feel that something is not right about them but you cannot explain it. Your subconscious helps you to be cautious. Possibly that person hides a dark secret, or is dangerous.

Your subconscious is connected with us, the Angels, as well. It is that part of you that communicates with your Higher Self who translates our warnings or guidance, back to you. To receive them, you must be in sync with yourself, to have peace and joy. Your conscious mind is surrounded constantly with thoughts and your ego self, that holds your blockages, and so it is difficult for you to translate the messages. The practices of this book try to reawaken you, to bring you in a deeper connection with this Higher Self and help you follow your intuition easily.

Anything that you see in a physical form that brings your awareness towards us, it is a sign to remind you of our presence. This could be anything from a child passing by, to a sound. Whenever you capture our signs, your intuition assures you; it alerts and assists you to translate it. Whatever you think these signs mean, you are correct.

In dream state we approach you easily. We may whisper to you solutions to a problem or guide you towards the next step to take. Upon awakening, when you clear your thoughts and energies, the answers flow.

Whenever you ask us for something, either an answer to a question, a material thing, for us to take care of others, even a sign or guidance, we always respond. The way you communicate with us or Divine Being, is easy as long as you hold your attention towards us. You can ask us at any time, any place and any way that is more convenient to you. It does not have to be formal, neither is it necessary for you to choose your thoughts or words. We are your siblings and we never judge you. We hear all forms of prayers as long as they have the clear, focused intention to be heard. Many spiritual beings, hear your pleas and all are available if you ask for help. Hold that intention in your mind and talk to us through your thoughts, words or even emotions. We hear you. All of us assist you in our own way that may differ from one another. Know you receive an answer to all your calls and prayers. Follow your intuition and feelings and you will get to our messages.

We are not fancy and we do not want formal introductions. We always respond to your pleas no matter the cause, form, or way they are communicated. You do not need to have a reason, just feel our love from within.

Know that a lot of other spirits want to assist you also such as Ascended Masters like Christ, Mother Mary but also fairies, Spirit Guides and many more. All of those use similar techniques to do so. Signs that we bring are endless but always come in such away to alert and not frighten you. We always bring uplifting energy and courage. Ask for our signs, and be sure you shall receive them.

We are nudging you towards bliss.

CHAPTER 13

BLESSINGS IN DISGUISE

This place you stand this moment is exactly where you should be. God has a plan for you, and everything contributed to make you the person you are now. Certain experiences need to occur for you to grow and expand, good and bad. Some of your experiences you chose before reincarnation and others you create as you walk along. Some occur to bring you expansion and lessons, while others to bring you changes. In this chapter, we help you understand the reason for all those changes.

Life-changing experiences exist to fulfill a purpose and expand you in knowledge, wisdom and strength. Perhaps you have lost your house years ago, but now you have an even better life due to that change. A family member passed away, to move as a spirit guide and guide you. A partner has left you, only for a better one to fill their place. The old makes way for the new. Change should not scare you, as it is natural means for growth and expansion. We understand the feeling of loss that may come with whatever you leave behind, but know if you keep an open heart and a positive state of mind, you are rewarded you with something better. All changes are there to move you forward in life.

Certain events you attract as you focus your attention on your environment, while bigger changes, – let's call them milestones, you added before reincarnation to teach you lessons. These events could be anything from a sickly son to a partner or the birth of a child, or even the discovery of a pet. An event may occur that reveals what you should follow in life or offers you a big sum of money to fulfill a goal. Consider this your enlightenment coming from you, before reincarnation. Each lifetime offers something new, either skills, power of character, courage or anything that expands your being. These events are life changing, and needed for your divine higher purpose.

Do not take it upon yourselves to undergo hardships, because there aren't any. All that you find in your way are blessings, but some are in disguise to show you the way or teach you a lesson. Everything has a value and energy, and your attention to them makes them grow and expand into the cosmos and bring events with similar vibrations. For this, try to find blessings in each circumstance, because there is always a positive higher purpose on all events.

Remember: where you stand, is exactly the right place to be.

Move forward fearlessly.

CHAPTER 14

CHAKRAS

This physical body you now stand in, does not limit you in any way, nor blocks your Divine gifts. On this material form, lay gates of unlimited power. Unravel them with us now.

Your physical body holds portals of connection with your spiritual self, and in this way, you are always linked. Through those portals, you receive unlimited assistance, ideas, inspiration and guidance. If you clear them regularly, your communication becomes distinct; on the other hand, if you hold blockages and resistance, you limit that communication. Your true self wants to communicate and guide you at all times, but you must allow it. Together you are one, and this is where your power lies. Most of you, close the gate of communication with your Divine self as you cannot see nor feel its existence. Your ego differentiates your Divine potential and power, and only recognizes and accepts your physical shield. But you are only half a shield without your soul, that is part of your

Higher Self. As your connection with your Higher Self enhances, you find your power, you become complete, happy, enlightened; you become spiritually awakened, and more powerful.

These links exists in the physical body and hide your power and connection with the Divine. Some call them "chakras." There are gates of connection with your Divinity. If you hold no blockages or resistance, you can receive our guidance directly. Chatter, fear, wounds or any negative emotions prevent your chakras from opening and block you from Divine assistance, as well as, cause you discomfort and detriment of your physical body.

Your chakras or spiritual connections, are on several points on your physical body, but you cannot see them, because they exist in your aura or energetic form. If your aura expands, your chakras do so, as well. When your chakras are cleared, you become whole, healthy, euphoric and powerful.

We present some of those chakras, and how they connect with your Divinity:

One chakra, is on the place above your head; it is the link to your Divine Self.

Another is on the base of your spine that establishes a link with Mother Nature, so that you stay grounded while in physical form. When you departure from your physical body, this link is cut.

Other is the third eye chakra, as you may know it. It is in the middle of your forehead and lets you receive mental images and perception.

The throat chakra, exists on your throat area and it helps you speak of your truth.

The heart chakra holds your intuition and truth.

Your Solar Plexus chakra is around your navel area and brings you ways of expression.

Your sacral chakra is below your waist and provides you with creativity.

Those chakras are your links with the Divine, with your spiritual self, and bring you power. Believe in yourself and your powers, find your truth and you shall find all the gifts hiding in your physical and spiritual form. You are blessed and powerful.

We wait for you to find out.

CHAPTER 15

EXPRESS YOUR TRUE NATURE

This is our advice to you: Be true to yourself and do what makes you happy; be free from boundaries and limitations. God does not judge by the difference of character, appearance or gender. God only sees the purification of the soul. We are all spirits of God and have all come together to co-exist beautifully. You are called to live free with no boundaries or restrictions as this is the way to be happy.

It has become known to us that some of you beautiful beings, are afraid to show your true self, either by fear of judgment or by the control others have on you. Society has created unjustly belief among the years that eliminates anything that contradicts the state of "normal." And so, some who are "different" in character, style, or expression have been judged and treated unfairly throughout many centuries. The perception of God is that we are all normal and equal, for we all have a spirit, and control energy the same way. He values equality and freedom, and declares that all subjects within Earth and all around shall live peacefully with one another, learn, and come to experience existence in all its glory. Humanity has taken a big downfall on this manner, because of discrimination that keeps away people who make "wrong" choices, or look differently, or respond differently than others. All of you have the same freedom to live given by God and none of His subjects hold the power to eliminate this freedom. None should be responsible for restraining the joy from others, let along their freedom to live and express themselves as they like.

Sexual preferences are one of those controversial subjects throughout many centuries. There is a reason behind preferences, style, manner and character that make one not so different than the other. God has created all of His creations sexless. This is true for us, Angels, we are not given a name for we neither male nor female, but all are the same Divine Energy with a Divine Cause. Then God created all the others souls and attended to them the exact same way. You were all born without a gender, and thus you have freedom to choose as you like. In one lifetime, one chooses to materialize as male, while in another as female. There is no exception to this rule and all can become anything and anyone they like. Sexes were created to bring forth a new way of life, as both genders experience life in different way. You came to experience life in different forms and benefit from all interactions and qualities, and in this manner you are allowed to experience them so. Genders were not created to formulate new life but enjoy life in various forms. If God had chosen only one gender, then it would be enough to formulate others. However, you have been given the choice to decide a gender before each reincarnation.

One may have chosen to reincarnate as male, but in being, they lived and walked as a female in other lifetimes. The fact that this soul lived life on Earth under different preferences marked most of their experiences, and it became natural for them to continue expressing themselves in the same way. There is nothing wrong with that, for they only follow their natural responses. In the next lifetime, if they choose to be again male for instance, preferences might change. You should all be free to enjoy life in any way that you feel is right and no one should tell you otherwise. Be free, live life as you want and live it by the words of God. If you do, you will be truly blessed and happy.

We do not vouch for those who act against the will of God. Spreading harm in one's way, causing others unhappiness; eliminating freedom and joy from the world goes against the will of God. If one does not harm another in any way with their choices, then they shall be free to express themselves as they like. Remember you are hurting yourself if you restrain your true nature and preferences.

Experience life in any way that you feel is right, and God and His subjects will love you all the same. You are asked to treat others kindly, the same as any other being that is a creation of God. Any difference that you may have, character, style, manner, appearance– you are free to express it, if it does not harm another. You are advised to put yourselves first. If you live in misery you cannot benefit anyone else. You all benefit yourself and humanity by living in joy, freedom and experience life in the most beautiful way.

We love you all the same.

CHAPTER 16

RELATIONSHIPS

Beautiful interactions come in one's lifetime, to lift them in spirit and assist them grow. You may attract positive people or negative with your attitude, but your spiritual family stand by you regardless. This chapter is about all interactions that you find in your path, physical or spiritual.

Sometimes, you are uplifted around people, friends, family; other times, you feel sad and alone; this is due to your own frequencies that either attract people, or push them away. Whenever you are uplifted, happy and well, people and experiences that match that frequency, appear more often. In the same manner, if you are blue or unwell you attract more of them in your surroundings. This is for all people you interact with, either a friend, family member, a neighbor or a person that passes by the street. Here is an example: You are in a positive frequency therefore that stranger that waits with you at the bus stop is very friendly, chatty and makes time pass by very fast. Now let's assume you weren't so positive lately, and so, that person at the bus stop, matches that frequency. They are in a bad mood, rude and make your waiting experience longer and uncomfortable. This is similar to your every day interactions. Set the tone earlier in the morning and you will be satisfied with people, interactions and events that appear in your day.

The more you hold positive frequency, the more people events and circumstances move to match you. Have you ever wondered why unwelcomed people usually find the most unwanted times to appear? This is because your frequency at that time matches them, their mood, or your attention towards them. Like attracts like. In the same manner, when you vibrate positive energy, the less of these people appear in your path. Notice this and you will see it to be true.

The people most close to you, the ones you call friends, family or even partner, are not random, and have not crossed your path out of a coincidence. These people joined your physical life, to offer you lessons, assist you move on or lift you up when you are down. Before you came into this world, you chose not only your Spirit Guides to assist you in the spiritual realm, but the guides that are in physical form as well. Both physical and spiritual guides are there to assist you in any way possible. Usually, they are in the form of family members or partners. Their interactions bring you uplifting energy, and teach you valuable lessons. Perhaps they are there to help you learn about forgiveness, and let go of past life wounds. Of course, they have their own life and spiritual path to attend to, but you are all there to assist one another. People that offer you pure, positive emotions like unconditional love, understanding, peace, security, fun and uplifting energy, entail you are in the presence of your physical guides. We are sure there are a lot of instances these people helped you grow, help you cope with a trauma or offered you a place to stay when you were in need. These people are there for support.

Spiritual family sometimes reincarnates as your physical family, or friends as well. Yes, you do have a spiritual family; they are a team of souls who have been together, involved in one another's life, either in physical, or in spiritual form, since the beginning of their existence. These spiritual family souls are called your "soul mates" and there are more than one for each of you. These souls are born together in the same realm and hold similar values and powers. They are your *close* brothers and sisters, for all souls are your siblings as well. When you are in the presence of these souls, you are uplifted and you feel a close connection with them in your being. This is because together, you have grown and learned and expanded. You lived together in physical and material life, and you benefit the most from their presence. They all offer you different energies and abundant ways to benefit each other. These soul mates or spiritual family members can be reincarnated the same time as you, and either be in your life as your true family member, or later cross your path as a partner, or a friend.

Set your happy mood to be surrounded with positive people and circumstances and only bask in love and uplifting energy. Know there are no limits as to where help comes from. You are surrounded by loving souls all the time, either in spirit or physical form, eager to assist and uplift you. Call upon them now if you must, and notice who turns up. Your spiritual and physical family are not a mistake; rest assured, that you are taken care of.

And you always will be.

CHAPTER 17

CHILDREN AND THEIR POTENTIAL

Boundaries and limitations are created by the human mind and that is where they exist. When you came into this world, you had neither expectations nor limitations. You were cleansed from them, to start new, choose your paths and create your own life. Growing up, you became adjusted with several beliefs that still exist in your being, and block you from expansion. Let's face them together to help you expand.

If you believe that you cannot be rich, how can you create it? If someone told you when you were little that it is almost impossible to be rich, you would believe them, thinking you could never be rich, or that you must undergo hardships to do so. And so a blockage is created, that does not allow you to grow rich. We tell you this now: It is easy to be wealthy and not a struggle at all; nothing is.

Children are of the purest and most gentle human beings that walk on Earth. They are more connected to their Higher Self, and they have purer energies. Before reincarnation, you have been temporarily cleared from blockages to start new and fulfill your life's purpose, and have a life full of love and joy. There, you began a new journey of creation with a peace of mind, and desire for knowledge. Since children hold no negative intentions and their conscious is blank, it begins to fill with anything they pick up from their surroundings. The notions and ideas children are presented with in this crucial period of their lives, is very important, as it makes them who they are, and what they will grow up to be.

Perhaps you grew up with strong beliefs about certain matters, that your family passed on to you. Those beliefs caused you blockages. Think of the example of racism, it is all relevant to the beliefs you were exposed to as a child. You, now, continue on that frequency by adding to those false beliefs and ideals, and create a life of struggle and in this case, hatred. The young are open to any perception they receive from their environment, and that's what makes them truly vulnerable.

You have your free will, to choose your beliefs, acts and ideals. We are not here to go against your free will nor tell you what you should or shouldn't do, but rather advice and assist you. We have pointed you towards this book, and we let you decide if you want to attend to it or not. You can go about your days without attending to what we discuss here and that is okay too. We do, and always will, love you no matter your choices, and no matter your beliefs; nothing will change that. All of you are free to do as you like and believe anything you pick up along your physical path. Children, on the other hand, create their free will, and choices, based on the bias and perceptions of their parents and environment. Help them to set them right, to bring beauty and love into their lives, as well as, save them from hardships and blockages.

Imagine the life you could have had, if someone told you many years ago: *"Being wealthy is easy and you can do it if you believe it is possible."* You would have taken different paths, made different choices; you would be somewhere different in your life, where struggle for money does not exist. You can give that advice to a child, and they will know it. It will save them the hardships and struggles. The world is truly magical, and if only someone tells you, you will be able to see it. Tell our little friends, teach them, too; they will adore you when they know. Remember the world is truly beautiful;

and you are too.

CHAPTER 18

MOVING THROUGH TIME AND SPACE

Due to the time limitation that exists in the space reality in which you reside, usually the cosmos does not respond to your thoughts immediately. It is also impossible for you to be in many places at once. Spiritual beings, on the other hand, are not bounded by time or space; so why are you?

Time exists to allow physical beings the ability to control their thoughts and thus, use their focused attention to shift any unwanted events from occurring. What would it be like if you put your attention on a fire, and immediately a fire is caught in your home? Not very convenient. And so, a time-line exists, to allow you to control your thoughts. The say way, when you add focused attention in a matter, you receive it back to you in Divine timing, when all events and people are ready for it. And so, time allows you to realize your thoughts, and shift them if negative to positive. As you practice controlling your thoughts, time limitations will not be a restrain any further, and you can materialize your thoughts faster and faster.

Astral projection gives you the ability to move through time, while being in the same place. It is possible, and it is achieved by many, but it requires skill, focus and guidance. Astral projection is not how we, Angels, move but it is similar, since the same focused attention is used to move your being in other space and time zones. Certain skills as the ability to keep yourself grounded, is needed to successfully astral project and return to your time and space. You succeed astral projection, with a focused attention to where you want to go, and by having a strong connection with your Higher Self. It is advisable to ask us for protection before you attempt to move in a different direction in time, so we keep you safe and show you the way. At the moment of projecting you must hold no resistance, nor fear in your being. For this, many of you achieve it unconsciously before drifting to sleep, or while in deep meditation. In both instances, you let go of anything that keeps you grounded and walk against the limit of time.

You can move through time and space once you become more skilled in controlling your thoughts and allow your being to expand and grow. Everything is possible in this world you stand; while you do have certain limitations that keep you grounded, you can move pass them. You can achieve unimaginable things from where you are: time travel, instant manifestations, astral projection, clairvoyance, psychic ability, empathy, enhancing physical skills such as speed, or stamina, and many more. All skills and techniques are possible if you find your true connection and control your focused attention. You are truly powerful, and if only you let yourself grow you will see it too.

Once you spirit awakens, time will move faster for you. You won't have a sense of time or limitations to hold you back; your manifestations will become instant, and you can acquire skills with ease. Control your thoughts and feelings, and return to your own power. You are so very skilled, if only you knew how. Believe, hold pure intentions, love whatever comes your way and trust that the universe will bring forth anything you sent out to it.

We love you, you powerful beings.

CHAPTER 19

LIGHT AND DARKNESS

You are the Light. God gave all equal attention and formulated souls out of lighted Energy. You hold this light within and as you grow, it expands; as you create, you use it everyday with your focused attention. You are a Lighted Being that forms good. Darkness comes to those who distance themselves from their pure nature and natural Light.

When you interact with the world, if uplifted, your energy multiplies. In this way, the more uplifted and happy you are, the more power you hold in your being; the greater Divine Light you carry. It is so pure that only good comes to those who hold a fair share. On the other hand, when you fill your heart with worry, fear and any other negative emotion, this Light constricts. The less you hold, the further you move from Divine Beings, good vibrations and experiences, and the more you limit your power and darken your life and surroundings. When you are in the dark, bad events, circumstances, people and beings with similar darkness, reach you and on and on it goes.

There is no such thing as evil, only beings with limited or no Light. Beings, without Light, either physical or spiritual, bring misery, worry and fear. The stories you believe about evil lurking in every corner, do not stand. Given by God, those who are away from the Light are surrounded with darkness and fear; due to the energies they hold.

Imagine a lighted room in a dark house. The closer you are to the lighted room, the more light you receive. In this way, if you hold Light and attention towards the good, darkness cannot harm you in any way. Dark beings are only lost souls that are blinded by fear and do not allow themselves to see the Light. The "devil" that many of you fear, does not exist, but souls who lost their way are plenty, and they exist in lower dimensions where Light does not reside. Angels, on the other hand, are only pure beings and always will be. You, physical beings of semi-dimension, stand in the middle of us and them and with your free will, you choose to surround yourself accordingly. If you hold pure intentions, joy and love in your heart, no one other than Lighted Beings surround you.

We do not want to scare you; fear is one of the things we are keen on. We reassure you that nothing bad can reach you, especially now that you are a holder of this book; if you apply the lessons we give, you will be surrounded by the Light. Know that: the Light and the Divine are more powerful than anything else. Even if you hold the slightest attention on us, anything else fears to approach.

God attends to all beings, and all are given the same White Light with pure energy and free will. With this free will all beings choose where to focus their attention, and what kind of energy they wish to have. Angels are given to all physical beings for protection, but if one is filled with darkness, Angels cannot reach them. At any time anyone can return to the Light, and they will be welcomed with so much joy and love. Those who remain in the darkness, however, do not want to be saved, restore their Light, or grow and experience happiness. They live against the will of God, and they are free to do so. If they do not want to be saved, we cannot intervene with their free will, and so they remain in the darkness. Those beings hold many negative energies, and the further away they have been, the more darkness they hold and bring to those who turn their attention towards them. In the same way, the more joy and love you have and give, the more Light you hold and bless those around you.

Enough with the darkness; we only want to speak to you about the Light. The way a candle's flame lights up the darkness, you are a light beam that empowers with shine. Remember: do not fear the darkness, for you are surrounded by Light that it is more powerful.

You are protected.

CHAPTER 20

THE GALAXY

What is the purpose of all those planets that surround earth? Same as Earth, the planets and the stars, hold other energies within, that you cannot touch or see, the way you cannot see our true angelic form. The universe holds many planets like Earth, that welcome various beings in different layers.

Gaia, or Mother Earth, is created to welcome physical beings to enjoy the plane of materiality. God has created many ways for one to live and expand, as God lives through them and expands as well. The Earth in this physical dimension, holds various advantages and disadvantages. Some of those advantages, entail taste to enjoy nourishment, vision to enjoy human form, earthy beauty and creations; human touch and sexual pleasure, gifts of materiality. All those only exist on Earth, and they are unique in their creation; they are the world as you know it in this lifetime. Of course, limitations exist as well such as: time, gravity, oxygen breathing every second and more. In this way, Earth is a paradise for those who learn to enjoy both their physical and spiritual form.

The other galaxies and planets welcome various other planes were souls, are reborn, or created to enjoy their own expansion. Human eye may not see nor comprehend them, but they all serve God's bigger plan for life. You fear of aliens, as that is something new you cannot understand. Fear not of all those souls that reside in other planes and galaxies; they may have different forms and limitations, but they are all a creation of one. The other planes do not worry for physical expansion, but they search for fulfillment within. Your planet is yours alone and will continue to be, with the will of God and Mother Nature.

The stars hold their own story. You see stars fall, but new ones are reborn. They fall because their shine limits, their energy fades but they are reborn again in other planes and galaxies. Nothing is lost, and nothing ever dies. The old welcomes the new, and on and on it goes. The stars and other planes lay in other layers of dimensions; some are close to Earth, some are far away, but all fulfill their own purpose. There are Angels and other souls that are assigned to look after those, as well.

You have visited other planets and know there is more than meets the eye. In all those planes, life is experienced differently. Earth has water, air and oxygen, while another planets do not; Earth welcomes physical beings that rely on those necessities while in others they live based on will and unity. You are unique, as you live in a material form while exploring your spiritual one, in another life you may do otherwise. You expand and gain new traits in this way. If one eats the same food and does the same things everyday they never learn anything new, they never expand. The same way you are moving and expanding, you never die; you are never in one place.

As you will notice if you take a look at the universe, God is font of change. Earth moves around itself and around the sun to bring new experiences of day and night, hot and cold. The stars fall for new ones to be reborn, humanity evolves and changes. The hair on you head grows, your height and weight change, the age on your skin shows. In nature the trees grow, create new leaves; even the animals change their fur or skin. There is change everywhere never endingly. Your natural state is moving energy through you and to you. Energy brings you new matters and ways, opportunities and changes. And so, the planets and galaxies move and change as well, if not in speed, in expansion. New galaxies are created and new souls are reborn in other planes; the character of the soul resembles the advantages of each plane they are born into. Some benefit with courage and kind heart, others with leadership and mercy. You are unique and never stop evolving and gaining new traits and skills.

Do not be afraid what you cannot comprehend; trust that all fulfill God's plan for expansion and life. You may not see it, but it is there, you may not remember it, but you have walked on other planes. You are unlimited and you evolve, you change, you learn. And so, all is formed the way it is, for all to benefit. The Earth moves and you do as well.

It is more fun this way.

CHAPTER 21

DIFFERENT DIMENSIONS

The world as you know it is a single view of how everything is. There are various other layers similar to your own that you cannot see nor comprehend. This chapter reveals the different layers of existence, or else known as "dimensions," that subsist within your own.

We, the Angels, exist in the 13th layer of existence, and we move freely in others'; for you, however, it is different. You can move in other dimensions, but only once you have completed the one you were assigned. When you return in spirit, you choose to follow another path, another life, perhaps in another layer of existence, so you too, are able to move through layers.

These layers, are different "places" that life exists. All of them have different qualities, and life is experienced in other ways than the one you know. On the third layer that Earth is, exist: time, space, gravity and as you call it "death," that is only the end of a lifetime, and marks the beginning of another. We, the Angels, do not exist in other dimensions nor do we reside in your own. We move in all other dimensions freely. We can even walk in physical form if we choose, if it is necessary to assist you, and we have done so many times already.

Other layers, or existences, hold different values and other frequencies. Time does not exist in them, and beings are more awakened to their power. They can move as they like, or they can communicate with each other with feelings the way we do: from within. All layers have their benefits and all beings have expansion to undergo and things to learn. When, at any time, you exist in those layers, you pick up new abilities and expand. As you return back on Earth in a later physical form, you hold more gifts and powers in your being. With this, we also remind you how much power you hold, as you do not come from one dimension, but from all the others as well.

You are powerful and unique, and you expand with every life and experience. God does not let one fall, or get lost if they want to be found. Ask for guidance and assistance, and we will be available to you in any layer of existence, in any form, in any galaxy, at any time. You always expand in any layer that you are, in any form that you live in.

You are powerful this way.

CHAPTER 22

CIRCLE OF LIFE

The material form you take in each lifetime, is based on the experiences you wish to gain, and the effect you will bring to others. Any physical form, that is alive, holds energy and thus a spirit. All beings have materialized for a purpose. Each material form contains all the necessary features that it needs to succeed, and to fulfill their Divine Purpose.

Animals and trees have souls of their own. Anything that exists and is living, is created the same way as you: First they were spirit, and then took a form to fulfill a task. They have powers and energy as well; they radiate frequency, expand, grow and fulfill paths.

What is the path of a tree or a fish? you wonder.
They radiate energy in different ways; they bring beauty, connect with Mother Nature, and succeed their own expansion. A tree

connects with Earth, that nurtures it, and provides for it, the stronger the roots on earth, the stronger the tree and the more energy it contains. Then the tree, itself, brings oxygen to continue the circle of life, gives you fruit, or food to the birds; it is but a valuable life to continue the whole. A fish gains skills from the ocean, grounds with Earth, and advances. In return, the fish feeds the birds, other animals and people; and so the cycle of life, continues. Even a seed, for instance, is a form of life on its own; it has energy and a purpose of becoming a healthy tree. For this, protect all beings as they come to gain life and fulfill their path as well.

Do not mistake an animal for something worthless or pointless, as they hold purity and power. Many of those species had or will have, a human form in another of their lives. One is not punished or degraded if they are in a smaller form. Do not confuse them as impotent because they are from that. All souls come forth willingly to provide for Mother Earth, continue the circle of life, experience a new way of living, and gain new skills. These beings, as small as you may think they are, live by purity and Divine Energy; they absorb your frequency and even share their own. The life of a flower or a mouse, are creations of God, that co-exist and advance. Every form, every galaxy, every dimension offers you something new, you always gain, no matter form or size. The more lives you have lived, the wiser you become, the stronger your energies get.

Should I feed from those animals? some wonder.

The cycle of life is for the bigger to feed on the smaller. Does a lion sin when it feeds with flesh? Does a chicken sin if it eats the worm? In the same way, you follow your natural instincts for survival. We do not ask you not to eat other species, but to respect them. Do not cause them cruelty, for they receive energies as well, and get affected. An animal came forth willingly for the purpose of continuing the cycle of life. They knew their path before they came forth, yet they wish to expand and experience whatever that life brings. Do not harm the stray cat at the end of the street, do not kick the neighbor's dog; respect all species, as they have as much right to be there as you. Appreciate all food before you consume it, for it has provided you and covered your hunger; it has fulfilled its purpose.

You are small, yet so big and powerful; even a flower gains and gives the way all of you do. Treat all beings with respect and love, and the universe will bring back to you through the law of giving and receiving. You are one form, but you came from many others. Each of that form matters, regardless the size; it makes your being more powerful.

You are unique.

CHAPTER 23

AFTERLIFE

You were always pure, and you will continue to be. You came with Light and Divine Energy, and so you will leave. Death does not exist, nor is the end; it only entails the end of an era, an extension of life which marks new experiences. In this chapter we explain the steps a soul takes after a lifetime comes to an end.

After a physical death, you continue to live as the soul never ceases to exist, and its journey never ends. You leave behind your ego and memories, as a chance to start anew and rejoiced. You leave behind anything that grounds you from that lifetime while you move into a higher dimension. We always surround and show you the way. We attend to your soul and hide misfortunes, troubles or trauma you have picked up from that lifetime. We also remove blockages and worries for relatives left behind. All that is left, is a loving awareness of all that you were and of those you know. You can attend to your loved ones to assist them to heal from your loss, and help them move forward. You choose who you will attend to, where you will go, or how to interact with physical beings. However, you are always bound to their free will, and you cannot intervene with their perceptions or troubles. You cannot fix their lives from above, as that it is neither your journey nor task. All you can do, is give them love and support and then move on to attend to your own expansion.

You can always make choices as your free will never ceases. You can select where you reincarnate next, what form to take, what journeys or paths to fulfill. Many souls have specific tasks to attend to: some serve humanity, while others to expand the self. Any life path you choose must undergo success in order to be removed from your path. And so, all of you continue to live, fulfilling your life's purpose and expanding your spirit. Upon completion of your life's path, you will rejoice in higher realms once returning to the nonphysical. You would have more energy and more gifts and so you can use your energy in more ways. Ascended masters are souls with high energetic power that have completed their life's paths.

Do not fear death, as it does not exist. It only means the end of an era and the beginning of a new one.

You came and depart in love.

CHAPTER 24

PROPHECY

You may call this chapter a "prophecy" of your physical world as it will be in many years to come.

As we explained in earlier chapters, the shift to the fifth dimension has already begun. This spiritual shift that occurs that affects you. You become awakened by the truth of All-that-Is, you are uplifted and more powerful.

The corruption and alienation of the now third dimension, shifts and expands into purity. Old patterns are replaced by new. Money is a form of that pattern that undergoes a crisis and will eventually shift, and transform into a new pattern that takes its place. You are not to fear, this is a blessed change that is needed to release humanity from financial slavery. You have altered the meaning of money, and many are born hostage of its ways. You put it first in many areas of your lives, and it controls all the rest.

Think of the children, and how happy they are not to bother with money, bills and debt. You are to meet them, living free and happy as money will control your life no more. The notion of money, and the exchange of labor to profit will change. A new way is in the means that brings financial freedom and establishes new patterns of giving and receiving. Finance will no longer be a problematic area as it will be resolved in peace. That entails the end of cheating, theft, and injustice with money. A better share will be established for all.

Medical studies are to rise and make way for cures and expansion into more areas of medicine. God ensures all of your desires are met, and that entails the decrease of illnesses and struggle. The world is created to thrive and live in joy, love and ease, and so it shall be. Illnesses will decrease and people will no longer suffer the way they do now.

Religions will no longer contradict one another. A common ground will be met for all to join in love. It is time to leave behind old perceptions and embrace the new. God is available to all, and created His beings to love and give and receive. No laws will contradict this freedom. Those that live against those ideals, will be reborn again and change those beliefs. The old perceptions are to fall away for new ones to arise and bring this world to unity and love.

Many old patters will shift and transform to serve well-being. New leaders will rise that will bring equality, freedom, peace and mercy. They are the leaders that people will embrace and know to be true. Few will be the ones that doubt them but even so, the mazes will know the truth. God sends you these leaders in many areas, not just one, and answers your plea for peace and love.

Technology and sciences will progress rapidly allowing you

to embrace your own power with ease. Teleportation, medium communication, and even flight are some of the ways you will meet the other galaxies in power. You will uncover your potential, and with that your power to do and be many things at once. Ideas, will be created to serve humanity, that are to be embraced and celebrated. The old makes way for more expansion that rapidly unfolds before you.

Corruption and evil doing will not cease to be, but it will be limited in energy as most of you will give way to the Light. As you do, you do not allow the darkness to rise and grow, and so it cannot affect you anymore. You are to be awakened, with more Light and Divine Power, and so the darkness cannot destruct you. With your rise, you leave the darkness behind.

There is no end to living and expanding, and there is no end to the world, for you are created to live and expand. There is only the end of the world as you know it, which entails the rise of humanity into higher realms of existence, closer to your Divine right, closer to God. Those who choose to remain in the darkness, will be left there with their choices, but the rest of you are to rise and expand, the way that you should. This is our prophecy, for we know and see how this world moves, and we are happy that you shall meet us in the Light.

The fall was in the past; in the future, there is ascension. The rise of humanity into a word of love begins, as more, and more are reborn awakened, and more of you will be too. It has already begun.

We know it to be true.

PART II:
CREATION

CHAPTER 25

THE WORLD IS YOUR OYSTER

"The world is your oyster." You can be, do, or have all that make you happy. This chapter, in an introduction to your power, to remind you of the abundance of things and experiences that you can have. You are worthy of all of them.

With your focused attention, you can achieve all that you desire. First, you must recognize the absence of the things you want, so you can create a desire for them. Once those desires are realized, they become strong and primary thoughts, so that they are added enough energy and desire needed to materialize. If you allow yourself to recognize all that you want, and not stay in their absence, the wishes will come to life basking you in love, appreciation and completion. When you recognize what you desire, you must let go of their absence so you can move into their presence; ask and then allow to make any desire come to life. In this part, we help you to recognize and experience them.

    You are abundant, not necessarily in the material world, but in spirit. Nothing is too difficult to create, since you are by nature a creator. The reason so many of you find it hard to receive your desires, is because you are filled with worry, fear and doubt. Come back to your true natural self, find your peace, bask in love and appreciation and you will see how easy everything would be.

You are unlimited.

CHAPTER 26

HOW THE UNIVERSE REALLY WORKS

As you embark upon this journey of self-discovery and creation, you become unlimited from resources that lay in your way. Those resources exist in your everyday experience, to assist you grow and expand, fulfill your desires and bring you power and joy. They are your own interactions, lessons and experiences that you have access to everyday.

All the information and data that you process, exist in your subconscious, and you have access to them at any time. They can be in the form of memories, emotions, sounds, smells or knowledge. All this information you process every minute of your lives, passes onto the subconscious and creates a link of connection with you and the cosmos. Let's refer to these connections as "cords." These cords exist in your being, and offer millions and millions of interactions and experiences that connect you with certain ideas, moments, people, events and even material things. Everything that you put your focus into instantly creates a cord that links you with that matter, at any time. A simple recollection of a person, for instance, is all that it takes for that person to appear into your experience. It is as if "you pull the cord" that connects you with that particular person, and like this, they appear into your experience. This is the same with anything that you put your focus upon. You can cause an event to enter your life experience, simply by recalling the image or the feeling of it. If you hold no blockages towards it, you will attract it into your life.

Try it now: Put your focus on a person, idea or a material object for several seconds. Experience it as vividly as you can, and you will ultimately see it in your life.

You are the one that moves the strings; you are the one that controls your life experiences. The universe is a "place," full of all the cords that people created throughout their lifetimes. These cords are available to all who attend to them, and can attract them into their lives. If a thought is attended to regularly it creates momentum that pulls the cord closer and closer with each process. The universe or cosmos does not have a mind of its own, it rather creates what you give it, as all have access to this "law." You call it "Law of Attraction" or "karma," and it is simply an understanding of how the universe works. It is but a law like the one of gravity that holds you grounded without any effort on your part, and with no exception to anyone that walks on Earth. The universe is a big "organism" that radiates energy that is controlled by you. Only you have access to the things you want to have and the experiences you want to get. Put your attention towards them, and they shall shift and move towards you.

The experiences that already exist in the form of memories,

can be more easily attended to than others, since all you have to do, is remember them. However, you have access to any other experience as well. You are truly unlimited, and so is the world you stand. The universe finds a way to respond to your focus, and it gives you a sign that it is under way. Anything that makes you think of your wanted desire is a confirmation that it will enter your experience soon.

Become aware of what you create at any moment, and choose the right experiences and thoughts to have. Be picky and careful with your thoughts and words because they do create your tomorrow. Do not give attention to what isn't beneficial so you do not pull those cords with unwanted events. And like this, your life will be filled with the beautiful moments that you attended to.

Be happy, be in control, master the skill of controlling your thoughts; it will serve you greatly. We believe in your power and know that all you learn today, will serve you in this lifetime and in others. See the beauty that surrounds you now.

You are truly blessed.

CHAPTER 27

WISH AWAY

We understand your need for improvement. If you had all you needed already, then you would not care to expand, and learn, and improve. The universe, through your life experiences, causes you to decide what it is that you want, and create a desire. There are times that you suppress that desire; you do not allow yourself to acknowledge it. In this way, you prevent it from coming into the surface and keep the cosmos from bringing it to you. Your desires are blessings; they are a way to improve and uplift; let them out, acknowledge them, invite them.

Why do many think it is false to wish and dream of new things to have? It is only a desire for new experiences. You must acknowledge wishes to bring miracles into your life, to materialize what you hold in thought, and to allow the universe to bring them to you. Let the ship sail with your desires and know it is, indeed, going to reach its destination. Realizing your desires is a very important step. How will you know what you want if you do not acknowledge it first?

Remember when you were just a child and someone asked you what you wanted to be when you grew up? Your feelings were awe, amazement and excitement for the future, because you had so many choices to select from. You felt the world was so abundant and wonderful, and the future so amazing that it was to yield to you all your chose. And then, you grew up. When we ask what you want to be tomorrow, do not hesitate; do not think that your wishes do not matter, because they really do. The universe wants to yield to you all that you want but first you have to create them. Your desires are God's gifts to expand you; accept them and fly.

The opportunities are endless and so are the experiences. Do not hold yourself back from them. Why do you think you deserve bad experiences? Why do you keep yourself from having beneficial opportunities? A phrase like "this is too good to be true," is what keeps it from being true, whatever it is that you desire. It is not wrong to want the beautiful experiences, nor is it selfish. We know you have many desires, wishes and dreams, and we are here to tell you, "Glorious." We want you to desire. It creates a happy expectation for what's to come. Wishes are a way of loving your life, and wanting to improve it. It is in fact healthy to desire.

Whatever you need to bring you joy is important to us, and to others. Remember, the universe has plenty, and resources are infinite. You truly can have all you desire. Wanting more is not greedy, if you share, and give others that of which you have. You may want a lot of money, rather than just enough, and that is okay. We do not judge, and you can have as many wishes as you want, to keep you satisfied; but, when they arrive, remember to be thankful and share joy to those around, as well.

Having it all, it is a lesson for others to follow. Your achievement is a demonstration for them to follow their dreams. For this, God is so fond of giving you anything that you ask. No matter how big or small, if it makes you happy, uplifts and resonates with your spirit, then so you shall have it, with God's blessings.

Do not be jealous of others' happiness or goods, because now you know that the universe is abundant and there are enough for all. Instead of jealousy, focus on that beautiful thing you just saw and admire it to attract it into your own life.

If you believe there are many resources for all, then you allow yourself to have more. If you believe that all should come easy, then so they will. You are God's beings and you will be blessed when you live in joy, love and appreciation.

In that regard, if one finds peace in whatever they do, if they are complete and in alignment then no one should keep from doing what they love. Not us, not family or friends. If one lives in harmony and love and never hurts another, God and all His subjects are instructed to let them be. No one should be responsible for taking another off their path, or keeping them from happiness.

Wish away, my loving brothers and sisters, and do not hesitate to ask us, and the cosmos for all you want to brighten your existence. You have lived through enough bad experiences; now it is time to allow the good ones to roll your way. Take a piece of paper and write down all your desires; find them, create them in the future; and then, you will no longer keep them away. Let them out. It is time to create.

Wish away.

CHAPTER 28

THREE STEPS FOR MATERIALIZING DESIRES

Once you put your attention into a matter, though, or idea, it expands by radiating your energy, and so it grows. If you do not give it energy, it remains as it is, and in time, it will fade and dissolve. On the other hand, if it is given enough energy, it expands into more layers of focus, and attracts other events in its way and ultimately materializes before you. You wondered over and over, what steps to take, and in what ways you can create your desires into the physical reality. To explain the materialization process we bring you this chapter.

The three steps you will need for a thought to form into matter are:
1. You discover what you want and why. Acknowledge that desire in detail.
2. Be positive, love your present moment and appreciate all

you have.

3. Do not worry for that desire any longer. Believe that the universe will yield it to you, no matter the way, and time.

Let's give you an example. Let's assume, you want a promotion at work. You have acknowledged this desire, and understood that you want it to earn more money. So, you give this event your positive attention, your energies are high and your belief is strong. You add so much momentum to it in this way, your frequencies signaled the cosmos that you are ready, and so you allow it to manifest. Everything is right, and in time, you will get that promotion. The manifestation then will be effortless and fast. On the other hand, if you are resistant in any one of the three, your desires feel stuck. Do not confuse this with right timing however, as certain events need to make way for others to arrive.

A thought, no matter big or small, if given enough attention, attracts circumstances that make it materialize in perfect time. But how you are doing with your desire? Is it well along the way, or is it stuck somewhere in between? Let's assume you want more financial abundance. Step one: You recognized whatever it is that you want, you wrote it down.

Step two: Be positive and happy in your present. Let's see how you are doing here. Think of the word "money" now. Then acknowledge what feelings you associate with that word. Go on, take a moment now before we move further and be honest. This is a time to reflect.

"Money."

Are your emotions similar to: A positive expectation, uplifting energy, abundance, joy, fun, plenty, rich? Or are they negative such as: Limited, low, stuck, anxious?

If positive, you are moving fast towards materialization, as those emotions define how you feel about that area of your life. On the same note, if you have negative feelings about your desire then you do not enjoy your life now nor believe you can have more. Money comes from you noticing they are not enough in your life, and so you create a negative response towards that area. If you knew you could have all the money you desire, you would not feel any negative emotion when you contemplated upon the word. On the same note, you do not appreciate all the money you have now, neither those experiences you gained with money. You only notice they are not enough. You must change the frequency of "money" to invite them in your experience. For this, we bring you many processes in this book, as you read along.

If your emotions about your desire are all positive, congratulations, it means your desire is so very close to you. Step 3 entails that you must allow it to manifest with your belief. Do you believe your desire can manifest at any time? Stay optimistic and believe that the cosmos will bring whatever you radiated. If you do not believe it is possible, this book will awaken you to see it so.

Test this exercise with any other desire you hold, and find out if you are stuck. Remember the universe receives what you are sending.

Change your frequency.

CHAPTER 29

YOUR DESIRES AWAIT

All exists for you to experience, recognize and appreciate. It is your free will to be, do and have whatever you desire. Do not hold back from positive experiences; the universe will yield you anything, as long as you believe. It is time to form those desires, that you hold at heart.

God gave you the gift to create your own life. For this, your desires are always met. When you say *they are too big for you, too good to be true, too unreal,* you do not allow those desires to be created. *Absolutely nothing is too good for you.* You are meant to be, have and do all that you put your mind into. Nothing keeps you from wanting them, from creating them.

Think of life as a magazine. You turn the pages one by one, and you decide which article or image, gets your attention to read or observe. If you give your attention to any article or image then it is created into your own life experience.

Try this in reality; pick an article or image and focus on it for a while, better yet, cut it from the page and put it on a place you see it often, and it will soon come to life. It may be in an hour, day, month or longer, but it will. In the same way, if someone says something pleasing and creates beautiful feelings, attend to it, give it your attention, talk about it, remember it; but, if it is not beneficial, turn the page, do not give it any emphasis. As simple as that, watch your life transform into a beautiful box full of magazine images. Your attention is the key to your next experience, use it well.

Create your life now, it is time you bring forth all that you desire. Write them in detail, find the pictures, feel the accomplishment like they are there, enjoy their energy. The universe will bring them back to you.

Do not worry about the how and the when: leave it all to us. Ask us to release you from doubts and worry that keep you from enjoying all the gifts you have chosen. They are all, now, underway.

The desires you created, have been received by the universe, that now works for their manifestation. There is no *if* they come, it is only a matter of *when*. No matter the blockages, no matter the time it takes, your desires *will* arrive. You do not need to visualize them every day, or keep asking for them. Let them go, they will find you. It is the law that God created. *You have asked and you shall receive.*

And so, your future is created. Do not think this is too good to be true. Why do you think life is meant to be hard? It is not, it really is easy and filled with many beautiful experiences; do not deprive yourself from them. Choose positive emotions, and so your life will be so. Read along the lines of this book and find many more processes to shift your attention towards a better life.

Your wishes wait to come to life.

CHAPTER 30

THE DIFFERENCE OF NEEDING AND WANTING

One of the reasons you reincarnated on planet Earth, is to have various physical and spiritual experiences. Spiritual beings, do not have the pleasure of materiality, but you are on earth to experience it. We will never call you greedy or selfish, since we understand that you live in a world full of beautiful paths and it is only natural to want to experience them. Wanting is a desire for growth, needing is a struggle from lack of the desired experiences. Neediness does not serve you, and it is time to let it go.

We know that most of you anticipate for all your desires to come to life, like a child waiting for Christmas presents. We love this eagerness, but the cosmos does not receive it as a positive response. Needing is a feeling that creates a negative significance, since those who need, are focusing in the absence of a certain matter, rather than to its positive expectation. Whenever you need something, you push it further away.

As you notice all the things you do have, you realize that you do not need anything else to bring you joy. Your life experience is beautiful as it is, and you should see it so, with all of the beautiful things you have in the present. Whenever you desire for more money for instance, you will think of all the beautiful things you can purchase with that money. This is a positive desire for wanting more to enrich your life experience. On the other hand, if you notice all those bills, and worry for not having enough money, the desire you create comes from your neediness. That desire focuses on the negative aspect of lack of money, and so you continue to attract lack of money. Hereof, when you want, you become a beautiful attractor of your desire; when you need it, you block that desire.

You dissolve the neediness when you focus on what you already have, and feel abundant. Look around; you will find many beautiful things that exist in your experience right this minute, rather than require another matter to make you feel abundant.

As we take a quick look through the eyes of our mediator, Amelia, for instance, we do feel her love for many things that surround her: the pretty little kittens playing next to her, the loving fiancé sleeping peacefully in the other room, the delicious pizza baking in the oven, the comfort of her chair, the anticipation of beautiful things to come. She is basking in the moment, and feels the beauty that exists in her experience now. A happy anticipation for more, as it comes from a feeling of abundance, brings more abundance.

Bask in the now and feel the love of anything that surrounds you; as you do, the neediness will fade and you will accept and love your life the way it is, and only anticipate for experiences to love even more.

Desire something, but do not stress over it; acknowledge your desire, but also, love anything that you already have, because the beauty lies in the present. As of this moment, you do not need anything, for you have so many things already.

    Love your present moment more than the next.

CHAPTER 31

THE POWER OF FOCUSED ATTENTION

Your ideas and thoughts cause a cosmic impact to all who walk on Earth because they are shared with all who lived or will live on your physical dimension. Anything you sent out, is available to all. The more energy a certain matter has, the more power, and the more effect to the ones who attend to it. Even the words you speak have an energetic influence.

As anything that exists holds energy, that energy can be transmitted to the surrounding people. A sick plant for instance, causes a negative effect to the people who notice it. If someone next to you cries, you draw part of that energy. In that regard, your energy gets affected with anything that you give attention to. Withal, you affect the energy of anything you attend to.

A notion or the meaning of a word for example, gains part of your energy every time you use it, and so it affects others who hear or use it as well. Focus on word of "love." It offers pure emotions that shift vibrations the more they are being used. Add that word in your vocabulary every day, and you will sense the impact of its positive energies matching your own. One word such as "hate" has so many negative connotations to those who have used it, and so it has a lot of negative momentum. If you use negative energetic words like this one in your daily vocabulary, you absorb them as well.

With the preceding information, we want to stress the importance of your focused attention, as even a word can cause your life to shift and change in the direction that you seek. This is one of the reasons affirmations and mantras work best. They hold powerful energy and the more they are attended to, the more they create positive energies, and invite them in your being, to match your own frequencies.

Notice the difference from admiring a flower blooming and a fire that destroys all in its path. If you shift your focus, look away, change the channel, you do not invite negative energies into your life. Similarly, when you surround yourself with negative people, events and objects, you invite their energy with your own.

Your environment radiates energies from all around. Focus on your attention and soon you will speak, act and see well-being into your life experience.

We love you so.

CHAPTER 32

THE UNIVERSE HAS A PLAN

So what if your desires have not materialized yet? This moment of your life, you are exactly where you supposed to be. The universe has a plan.

Nothing is random. Things come together to bring about synchronicities and more ideas and interactions that will contribute to the bigger picture of your manifested desire. It is alright if one matter has not come about yet. It means, you are not ready. Sometimes there are lessons to be learned that need to be acquired to help you make use of your desire in a deeper level.

Perhaps you worry or fear, and so the universe does not manifest your desire, because you are not ready to appreciate it. With those negative vibrations, you will recreate the same feelings and circumstances in your present. The universe protects you in this way and ensures you enjoy them in the best possible way. Once you resolve that fear, worry or anxiety, you will be ready.

If you are not emotionally ready to handle a sudden overflow of financial abundance, you will spent excessively, making hasty decisions and investments that will bring negative results. The universe ensures that you, and the other people involved, are emotionally ready for such a change.

Moreover, if you may have asked for a desire that is going to affect those around you, the universe makes sure they are prepared too.

The universe works with "Divine Timing." One event must move, in order to bring forth your desires. Here is an example: You want a new job. You have asked the universe that knows exactly what job is the best for you, but a woman is in possession of that job. The universe needs to take care of this woman first. She would soon realize, for instance, that she wants to travel the world, and so she asks to resign. Once she does, the universe will show you the way to get to that job. This is Divine Timing; you need to patiently await for the results to appear for you.

Another true example of Divine Timing, is with Amelia, our loving mediator, who desired a partner. A loving person, that will bring forth all these new experiences for her. The universe took a note of all her descriptions and knew exactly a person for her. But you see, this young man was with another at the time Amelia made the request. A month later, this woman broke up with him. This event needed to occur in order to bring those two together. This young man thought the universe worked unjustly for him, keeping the first woman away, but you see, he didn't know that the universe had other plans for him, and a life so much better with Amelia. And so, in this way, the universe brought them together, several months later, when they were both ready for it. What you are asking for is being given to you, but you need to be patient and trust that all is working out in your favor.

The universe works behind the scenes for you, even if you cannot see it yet. Trust that all is for the best, and leave the rest to the universe and to us. An easy technique for you to soothe your anticipation is to write a list of the wonderful things that you already have, and make this moment perfect for you. For instance, write and appreciate that you have your basic needs met, and so it is okay to wait a bit a more for the universe to bring you your share. You are fine in this moment; you are exactly where you are supposed to be. Whatever you are asking for is well on the way.

Do not worry or stress if your desire is not yet there; instead, know it is for the highest good of all, and it shall appear when you, and all involved, are ready. This moment is always where you should be, even if you hold resistance, it is alright; you are getting there. The universe sends you the best at the right time. Do not worry or stress or wonder how or when or if, but know it is coming. You are at the right time, the right moment, the right place.

>   You live in the master plan called universe.

CHAPTER 33

LIFE REVIEW

If we were to ask you about your life up to this point, what would you tell us? Give it some thought now. Remember all those memories, experiences and lessons you had. Were they valuable? What is your life story? Talk to us, we hear you. Are you happy with how your life has turned out? What memories do you recall? Give us your true response; recall your past and present until this moment. Spend time with your thoughts; it will truly be life changing. When you finish this task, then continue reading further. This is a life review of your life.

    What emotions did you bring up? There are no right and wrong answers, just the truth. Did you recall all those happy moments that passed you by, or did you remembered the hardships that brought you here? Both good and bad, happy or not, all of those events have marked your life story so far. Whatever images, memories or experiences you recalled during this time, were the events that marked you the most. They were your lessons, they made you stronger, taught you values, made you who you are. If it weren't for those events, you would be a different person. They have brought you here now, to create your new, beautiful life story. Your childhood, your old friends, school sweethearts, hardships, bruises, teachers, pets, houses, jobs, accidents, struggles, partners, joy, laughter and tears; all those were a part of you until this point. No matter how much you struggled, no matter the hardships, or the beautiful memories and experiences, they are all in the past. Now is the time to let them go.

This is the point that marks the end of an era. Your past is now gone. You have reviewed it, and it was necessary for what comes next. You now accept it, acknowledge that it has served you but you do not need it anymore, release it. Stop going back to that story, to these experiences. Stop beating the drum of who you were, because now it is all over, gone.

The old needs to make way for the new. How can you bring new experiences if old ideas still linger in your being? When you constantly recall old memories and blame them or wish they come again, you keep yourself from going forward. Stop looking back to what was; the new is much more exciting and awaits you now. It wants to be seen, but you are too busy looking in the past. Now you start new. The old is behind, but there are many more beautiful things to come. You have turned the page. Imagine a new chapter with blank pages that you fill the way you want. This is your life now: a blank page. There is nothing from the past that marks these pages. It is your new era. Make the best of it.

Say: *"I accept who I was. I am thankful for all those things, people and events that were in my path up until today, because they helped be who I am now. I release, and let go of the old, so the new can make its way to me, with better experiences that only bring loving emotions. I am ready to welcome it now. I say goodbye to the old and hello to the new. And so it is."* Like this, now you begin again. Let your new era begin. You are ready.

This chapter brings about new energies for you. It allows the old to wash away and the new to be created. All we ask is for you to stop looking back. There is nothing keeping you there anymore. You may have loved who you were, what you had, you may have not; either way, you start again, for a better life. The time is now. You are more ready than ever to start your life anew. All you create now will be: Create your story and do not bring about old perceptions or ideas, for those are in the past. Here, now, all is new and you make them as you like. So wish away and your desires shall come to life.

Your new life begins.

CHAPTER 34

WHEN TO ACT

How do you allow your desires to manifest? If the timing is right, you have no blockages and a firm belief that it will arrive, what is next? The answer is easy: You go with the flow.

Allow yourself to be taken to the right moment and to the right place. Go where synchronicities take you; act when it is time, when you feel ready, when you are sure. If at anytime you are hesitant of whether you should act, don't. Hesitation is the answer that it is not the time to act. If you are unsure, you are forcing an event to happen and it will not work. On the other hand, if you have an unstoppable urge to do something or say something, do so. It is time.

You, our beautiful physical friends, think a lot. When an idea comes, you over-think it in your mind and then doubt whether it is right or not. Stop it: this is when you misinterpret the signs and get confused. The answer lies in the feeling. If an idea comes to you, it excites you, it makes you celebrate,; you are sure about it, then you must follow it. If however, you over-think this same idea, the more you convince yourself it is not right, and you keep from acting. Similarly, there are times you persuade yourself that an idea is right. This means, you follow a thought with rationality and not with inspiration. Inspiration is combined with a positive emotion. You have to figure out what comes first: emotion or thought. Action that is Divinely guided in the right time, comes suddenly and is accompanied by strong positive feelings and urge to act, also known as inspiration. Whenever you get this you should act upon it; it will bring you positive results. On the other hand, thoughts that create an action and force a feeling to arrive, is only the ego self or your urgency, trying to create results, and this way, you will not bring your desired results. And so, differentiate what comes first: inspiration or ego, emotion or thought.

Trust your intuition; you know the answer already, and it will take you whenever you want to go. When it is time, you will know.

Trust your feelings.

CHAPTER 35

A LETTER FOR THE FUTURE

If you are optimistic and happy about your present, if you hold positive expectation for what is next, your future will be merry and bright. For this, we advise you to be blissful in the moment, trust that all is well and will be well along the way. When you have this knowing at heart, all shall fall in place for your highest and greatest good. With this chapter we help you reach that positive mindset needed for a happy tomorrow.

The future is yet unknown, even to us. We do not know something that has not yet been created with your attention. Once you have focused on it, it becomes known to us, and your future becomes created. Nothing is set in stone, as all of you have free will, and opinions to make your own journeys. Let's say somebody told you long ago, a so called "fortune teller," that you are to walk a path of struggle and difficulty. If you go with that perception in mind, then you create it so. If, however, you believe that your future will be merry and bright, then so it shall. We do not say that fortune telling is not accurate, for there are some people and various techniques that are truly blessed with that gift, but you need to understand that no one can know the final result, as you are the only one who creates it. One may read the energies you have put out there until now, but of course, we have taught you how to change those energies if something is not pleasing. Once you change your belief and attention, then these energies change as well, and so does your future. No one knows how you think and what your destiny will be; no one but you.

You may have chosen certain paths for yourself before you walked on Earth, but it is up to you to follow them. Destiny as you call it, is only in some ways predestined with events that will mark your path; but they are positive paths that benefit you or others greatly. Events like that are life-changing, like an event that reveals your life's purpose or the age you will reside from that lifetime. Big events like these are sometimes predestined, but they too, can change according to your path. Fortune tellers or even us Angels, cannot know the distant future because it is not created yet by you. What may be foreseen are only outcomes that might appear if you follow the same path and ideas.

Have you thought what your life will be like in 5 or 10 years from now? Why don't you create it now? Write your life story. Take a pen and a paper and compose it, then we would know, too. Remember to create something beautiful and fulfilling for yourself and others. After you are finished, put it in an envelope and keep it somewhere you will find it several years from now. Most of it will be true. Remember: believe it will be true, otherwise you may lose the opportunities as they happen. Keep a positive attitude that your future will turn out fine, and so it will be.

After you have composed the letter, you will feel a relief and positive anticipation for what's to come. That emotion is needed for it to arrive. This future is yours. Write it, know it, believe it and it is coming. Your letter has been shipped to the universe, and it is on its way to you.

Get excited.

PART III: RELEASE

CHAPTER 36

WELCOME YOUR NEW LIFE EXPERIENCE

Your attention creates your desires that manifest into your physical reality; unfortunately, your attention also contradicts them. With this chapter, we want to help you realize how you unconsciously block those desires from manifesting in your experience.

You are a Divine being that by nature radiates pure energy and holds good intentions. As you struggle and fear, you create blockages that bring you worry and unworthiness. Blockages are some of the negative beliefs you have picked up along your material experiences, that made you believe that certain things are hard to get, limited, do not come easy, are too glorious, large, or too good to be true. Thoughts such as: "*You are unworthy of what you want*" or that "*it is impossible,*" are only some of the thoughts that limit your belief and block your desires from your life experience. Those contradicting thoughts are captured by the cosmos and are welcomed events. Unconsciously or not, you tend at these false ideas that enter your subconscious ... your desires.

As you start your day; you hold no resistance, since no thought is being processed in your dream state. However, you do have thoughts; your mind flies from thought to thought, memory to memory, and processes all information that is given during the day. Then, all that information is stored in the subconscious, and only some passes in your memory. All of the ideas, thoughts, conversation and emotions are never lost, but always captured. You may not recall them, but you have unlimited information in your mind already, and some of them hold your blockages that are automatically brought up when a similar idea or event appears in your way. In other words, the subconscious is where you store responses from anything that crossed your wake experiences.

You have the power to alter and eliminate those blockages from your experience. The more you repeat those ideas, the more effect they have in your experience, and so it becomes harder to remove them. For this, it is easier for some, to continue believing they are real. They are absolutely not real. It is time that those emotions are brought into the Light and become eliminated. You, are only worthy of the things you desire: let them all come.

Read out loud, these few sentences and focus on the emotion they bring out:

"I am an unlimited being of creation and I create my everyday experiences. I now acknowledge this power that I hold, and choose to shift it towards joy, love and appreciation. The desires I want are ready to enter my experience. I accept why they haven't made their way towards me yet, and I now, consciously remove these limiting beliefs that kept me from those desires. I choose to live a life full of beautiful experiences, financial and spiritual abundance,

abundance of loving interactions, of health and wellness, and of the truth of who I really I am. I am capable, I am worthy of those new experiences, and I now allow them to enter into my being and into my life. I do not contradict them any longer. I am eager, loved, worthy. I am abundant. I create my own experience and I choose to fill them with joy, love and all those material and spiritual things I seek. I am now ready for a new beginning, a new life experience. I let go, I allow. And so it is."

Sit back for a moment and relax. Enjoy the peace that comes from the acknowledgment of these words. Allow yourself to bask in their truth. Allow yourself to remember who you are now. You are a worthy being of love. Enjoy the reassurance that comes from your being as you awaken the natural flow of positive energy and love, to enter into your life. Well done. We are truly abundant, and you are too. Welcome into this awareness; it is going to change your life.

Attend to these words regularly, and always remember who you really are, let yourself wonder with the pure emotions that these sentences bring. In later chapters, we guide you to completely remove those limiting beliefs, but for now, the acknowledgment is just as powerful.

This is the beginning of a beautiful experience.

CHAPTER 37

HOW TO FOCUS ON YOUR DESIRES

You beautiful physical beings, have a tendency to try and control reality. You focus on the ways a desire will enter your life. Alas, when you focus on the way, you do not bring that desire any closer to you; but push it further away.

If you give a painter directions as to how they will make an artwork, you limit their inspiration, imagination and the variety of choices they can produce. If you give them only the theme, they will create an inspiring work of art. In the same way, when you instruct the universe as to how you want your desire manifested, you limit the ways it will materialize. You do not let the universe work its magic. By wishing the way you'd like a desire to come about, you limit your expectations, and you do not allow it to come through the door, but through a tiny window. Deciding on how a desire gets manifested, is not your work. Allow us and the universe to bring it to you, in the most beneficial way, and you will not be disappointed. The universe is truly abundant, and the ways a matter can be created are truly abundant as well. Big financial wealth for instance, cannot only be achieved from a jackpot lottery or an inheritance, but from a bank error, an inspiring idea, or an internet transaction. Put your faith in the abundance of the cosmos and will beautifully surprise you. We understand your kind intentions but do not limit your manifestations. Form the desires and release them.

The cosmos does not need any help; just a thought is enough. If you focus longer on an idea, it is okay but do not struggle nor stress because it will not materialize easy. Let it go, let the intention wonder, let it add momentum on its own. Let your expectation and neediness out of the equation and then it will beautifully materialize.

There is nothing keeping you from creating a castle and a palace; it is all so easy and blissful as you learn to control your attention.

Find the things you desire and tell us, and the cosmos, with your focused attention. Relax, know all is well and taken cared of, including the ways and the how's. We love co-creating with you. We bring forth what you have summoned; expect miracles to enter into your life soon.

The universe is truly unlimited, and so are you.

CHAPTER 38

REMOVE BLOCKAGES

Beliefs that come from your limitations, worries and fears get in the way of your desires; you may have picked them up from your environment, or even your own negative experiences. Know that those limiting beliefs have served a purpose for you, brought you to this moment, and made you who are now.

Every day, you transmit frequencies that are sent out into the universe, which sends back equivalent frequencies with Divine timing. If you hold no altering beliefs or blockages, then they move right into your experience. If your beliefs block them, they become stuck in the energetic reality.

In order to release the blockages that exist in your subconscious, you must replace them with new thoughts that do not contradict your happiness, and whatever you want to attract. Since those beliefs were a part of who you are now, in changing them, alter a part of you. If you change a belief, your responses change as well. You will no longer be thinking, speaking, or acting in that negative manner. Be ready to let go of those perceptions and shift all your limitations, perceptions, fears – even negative people and circumstances. As you detoxify your being from all that does not serve you, you transform yourself and your life. If you are ready for this change, use the process of this chapter to let go of those blockages.

We instruct you to do this exercise for every area of your life that needs improvement. Let's begin our example with the area of health. Write on a piece of paper all negative beliefs that you hold regarding this topic. Sit in quiet and clear your mind from thoughts. Ask yourself: *"What beliefs, limitations or blockages do I hold for this area of my life?"* Then write down anything that comes into your mind; do not over-think, just write. Your thoughts will become clearer and more focused. Your Higher Self assists you in this process by helping you acknowledge any negative beliefs.

When you finish, read them and accept them as your negative beliefs. Those beliefs keep you from a desirable outcome and so it is time to remove them. Invoke us, the Angels to assist you in releasing those false beliefs. Simply state:

"Angels of the Light, I ask you to come forth right now and help me clear up those false beliefs and replace them with new ones that do not contradict my perfect state of being into the area of health. Thank you, and so it is."

When you ask us, the Angels, we are on the way to you. Acknowledge our presence surrounding you. You may feel tingling sensations or warm emotions, or even a knowing of our presence; all are true. Imagine all those beliefs rising up from inside your body and moving from your belly up, slowly to your throat and then out of your mouth. You may get a gagging sensation, or yawn, or even feel nauseous. That is alright; embrace them in any way they come up as it is the way for them to be realized and removed. As this process is over, sit on your list again and rewrite it with the opposite thoughts. If for instance you wrote: "*I am unwell,*" replace it with: "*I radiate joy and well-being and I bask in absolute health.*" Do this for all of your false beliefs, and then read them out loud. Know that the Angels are in agreement. Feel those new beliefs enter your subconscious.

"*And so it is.*" Say this sentence when you are done and go about your day relaxed, knowing that all is well, and nothing stands in your way of anything you want to achieve. You may feel lighter; or more aware of opportunities flowing into your experience; that is a sign of a work well done.

Have an open heart and be ready to release anything that does not serve you. We love you, bless you, and wish you to have a joyful day.

And so it is.

CHAPTER 39

DENY LIMITING BELIEFS

As you raise your expectations, you create miraculous things. If you believe something is unachievable, difficult or hard, you charge limiting vibrations that block you from receiving your desired manifestations. A way to release these false notions is to rewrite them from your subconscious.

How can you release the beliefs that give you struggle? How can you set new ones into motion? With the exercise of the previous chapter, you became aware of those blockages, and formed desirable statements to replace them from your subconscious. For this to occur, attention and repetition is required. Every time you recognize a belief that does not serve you, deny it. When someone tells you *"money is hard to come by,"* deny it. Replace it in your mind with *"Money comes easy to me."* Beliefs like that come about again and again into your experience in order to be released. When you agree with them, you continue adding them, but if you recognize they do not serve you, you can replace them. Pay attention to your thoughts in order to notice and renew them.

"*I need to work hard to earn my pay.*"
You recognize this is a false limiting belief; instead of agreeing and adding more momentum, imagine it emerging from you and out into the universe.
Mentally add: "*It is fun to make money.*"
And like that, you release it and add a new one. In time you would have cleared up all false beliefs by denying them, and new positive energy will take their place.

This activity requires your attention in whatever thought appears in your focus. Your subconscious may bring up those thoughts to delete them, so pay attention to alter them.

It is time for a release.

CHAPTER 40

FEAR IS AN ILLUSION

When you mask your fears, you allow them to remain within. Fear is not welcome, dearest friends. Remove it to be free.

You fear of evil, but evil does not exist. You fear of sickness, but there is only health. Your fear of death, but you can never die. Fear is but a creation of the mind; it exists only because attention is given to it. All matters are but an extension of well-being. Fear is further from love, evil is stepping away from the Light, sickness is to rediscover health, and death is but a beginning. One exists only because the other does also, and you have the choice to stay in one or the other. Do not chose fear; you do not belong there.

When you fear, you allow negative events to darken you. As you remain in lack, you do not allow abundance. Any negative experience you may have had, exists to bring you the opposite. In this regard, fear exists to move you back to love. There is nothing to harm you if you do not give it emphasis. God created you whole and pure and happy, and gave you free will. If you stay in love, fear cannot touch you. There are lessons to teach you values; give you strength, and show you the way to love. You are pure and holy; you come and exist in love.

Once you acknowledge fear, release it. Fear may exist within consciously or unconsciously. Perhaps it was created in childhood or through a memory, an event or the suffering of another. Some of those experiences you remember, others you do not, but all must be removed to return you to purity and love. Start with the decision to consciously remove fear. Acknowledge what is bothering you, recognize the purpose of that fear, make peace with it. Accept that those fears cannot harm you any longer. You do not belong with them; you are by nature in love, health and abundance.

Know we are always there for you for empowerment and courage. Ask us to assist you reveal those fears to consciously release them. Whenever you recognize an unwelcomed feeling, call us and we will surround you with love, restore your faith, soothe you.

Know all happens for a better cause; even if you do not see it, trust there is always one. Transform those fears to love, wellness and abundance. Remember: Fear is but an illusion of the mind. Nothing can harm you, for you are Divine and powerful and you have us by your side.

Be fearless.

CHAPTER 41

LEARN TO FLOAT

We know you have courage in your heart. We watch you struggle every day to survive. But life is not about survival and struggle; it is about peace and joy. When you stop struggling, you will float. Do not try hard to make things happen, to live by another day but enjoy, thrive and succeed.

We know your fears and doubts; we hear all your prayers, and pleas. Brothers and sisters, do not struggle; let go of all past experiences and hardships, so you can thrive. Release the pain, forgive, surrender to the power of the universe. If you let go, you will rise lighter, stronger. The natural flow of the universe is toward blessings and abundance. If your world is filled with negative experiences, you cannot see it. We are sad by your struggle. It is like a child drowning that you cannot save; we shout at you to let go so you can float; the waves will take you up if you do not force your way.

"*But how do I stop if my kid is starving?*" One asks us. You believe is neither the will of God, nor the universe that this child is to stay without food. Know and trust that the universe will provide; as you are sent there to live, and not to struggle for life. Your faith is your power; your courage is your will. If you let go of the misery, you darken your life no more. See the Light so it can find you and illuminate all within and outward.

Understand that it is not God's doing that you strife, but your own. You create your limitations and blockages that darken your soul and faith; alas, we can only help you if you allow us. Release your fears and let go of the struggle. Once you do, you will float and your wishes will be met. Think of a sea of waves; the waves have one direction, always; if you swim towards them, you move faster; if you go the opposite direction you struggle and never reach your destination. If something is stressful and makes you unhappy, change it.

"*Do I quit my job because I struggle? Will the salary come then?*"
Quit your job if it makes you unhappy, if it is what you do not want to do, if it does not fulfill you, if it causes you misery; but be aware: Do not quit something if the thought of no job, or no steady salary brings you more misery at heart, for then you will struggle some more. Act when you feel it is right, when you trust something better will turn up for you, when it feels safe and right, when you have faith. Otherwise, do not go against what you believe, for you will face struggles. If that job does not make you feel good, but quitting it brings you more negative thoughts and emotions, find ways to love what you do. Enjoy it as much as you can, convince yourself it

will get better and it will.

    Let go of struggle and you shall float. The universe works in mysterious ways, but only for those who believe.

Do you believe?

CHAPTER 42

LEVELS OF ENERGY

Set your schedule from early in the day, arrange your priorities and give yourself time to play. Allow time for regular breaks within the day to sit in peace, and restore your energies, so you have a day full of creativity, and serenity. Do not hesitate to step away from the masses when you feel the need, and always remember to breathe and be in the moment. Embrace a life of fun, love and positive experiences. In this chapter, we stress the vibration - energy levels, and their effect in your life. The more you hold positive energies, the more positive experiences you receive.

There are some emotions that are more powerful than others and affect your life in a deeper level. They can be positive and negative and we analyze them now.

The most negative emotions are: Distress, resentment, worry and fear are of the lower layers of energy that bring you unwelcome emotions and circumstances. Whenever you are in that state of being, change the sequence, do something else to distract yourself from that feeling: meditate, go to sleep, or color; in other words, engage in a fun, distracting activity until you ease those emotions.

Whenever you become fearful, calm yourself down by thinking reassuring thoughts such as: "*It is alright, everything happens for a reason, or everything will work out in my favor.*" This way, ease the negative emotion until it dissolves.

Other emotions of low energy brings you: doubt, anger, jealousy or anything that does not resonate with your being. Give those thoughts a farewell and replace them with positive ones. Do not attend to them any longer because they invite similar energetic events to join you.

Hope, serenity, fun, expectation, and any other positive emotion that offers you uplifting energy, is a high frequency emotion that expands your mood and frequency. Keep those feelings longer, and enjoy their power. Use positive words more often, and embrace activities that calm you and make you feel good. Some of them may be bird watching, listening to music, meditating, drawing or any other hobby you prefer. Spending time alone works too, assuming you enjoy your own company.

The stronger frequency emotions are the ones that make you feel reassurance, Divine Love, euphoria, peace, appreciation, comfort, and a knowing that all is alright. You know they contain a stronger frequency from the strong emotions they provide. A powerful feeling can alter your focus for the better, and render a radical shift of warm emotional energy. The more of those feelings you have, the more you set out your energy into frequencies that match them, and bring about joyful replies from the cosmos.

THE TRUTH OF ALL THAT IS

As you give more focus into the way you feel, you can shift anything to a positive emotion that will bring satisfying experiences. Do not give way to unwelcomed emotions but ask us to assist you clear them and replace them. You are a beautiful being that is created by love and pure energy to radiate and give love and pure energy. Attend to your thoughts and frequencies now, and become better with each stronger positive emotion. Do not limit yourself for anything less than feeling good.

You deserve only happiness.

CHAPTER 43

EMOTIONAL RESPONSES

You have come into this world to create. Every thought you form, every move you make, any topic you discuss vibrates energy that creates momentum. The more positive momentum you give to something, the more pleasing it will be, and as such, a negative attitude, brings unwelcomed results. Attend to your thoughts with an open heart and a pleasurable emotion such as: love, devotion, passion, appreciation or eagerness to create a positive momentum.

Altering your responses beforehand ensures that anything you attend to will bring you positive outcome. For example, let's say that in a gathering, you overhear people say that *"crime is all around in your neighborhood, and that recently lots of people have been robbed."* You are in the conversation whether you want to or not simply by overhearing it, and so with your attention, your energies are also. Quite possibly, you will pick up negative responses such as fear or worry and so it is better not to join the conversation, but alter the response in your mind. Assure yourself for instance, how this cannot happen to you, as you always lock the door, or that you have a dog to alarm you. Create a reassuring thought that offers you the opposite response of security and peace. In that way, you will not pick up negative energies from the surrounding conversation, but you will ensure a steady flow of security and peace. Even if you unwillingly find yourself in a negative emotion, alter it before it continues.

A girl contacted Amelia few days ago, worried for her exam results. She stated that *"Statistics declare foreign students only have 20% pass rate."* She asked to be supported by the Angels to write well. Statistics do not make the outcome, you do. You can turn any result to match your own positive responses. Amelia urged this girl to create her own destiny and not believe what others created for her.

The same is about all: do not rely on what the masses say or believe, but make it the way you want. So what if only so little or no one was cured from a specific disease? That does not mean you cannot. Anyone can do anything if they create their own positive responses. Do not say *"I can't,"* or *"It is impossible,"* because it is not. Responses make you who you are and who you will be. Bring positive emotional responses to anything in your life, and it shall be filled with abundance and positivity. Step away from the masses and how everyone else thinks; create your own response, believe it, and so it will be.

Whenever one believes they are beautiful, others, and the cosmos, pick up on that frequency and respond accordingly. The same is with being rich, poor, healthy, abundant and so on. Make your own beliefs about the world and yourself, and others will follow; the universe will respond.

Be aware of your responses in any topic or circumstance to ensure a steady flow of abundance and well-being, and so it shall be whatever you make it.

You are healthy, wealthy and loved.

CHAPTER 44

A MANIFESTATION TECHNIQUE

You will soon walk the path of your chosen desires. In this chapter, we help you bring them faster. Contemplate several moments a day over those beautiful experiences, to welcome their feeling in your present moment. Imagination is a powerful tool, and when combined with belief; it creates miracles. This minute is all you need.

Imagining your desires, creates pure positive emotions that give their energy momentum, while they bring you the feeling of accomplishment. In that moment, the gap of their absence dissolves. This notion of fulfillment sends out that frequency into the cosmos, by telling it you are ready to receive, and thus opens doors to let it in. Attending to this feeling of completion regularly establishes a common ground from where you are to where you want to be, and so it allows it into your experience without any blockages.

Use the gift of imagination for your benefit. Let's get you in the receiving mode now. With eyes shut or open, focus on the environment shifting, and replace it with what you wish to see. Pretend like you are a child playing, and do not worry if you seem silly; this is a great tool to assist you towards the life you want.

What if whatever you wish for has materialized here, now? In this moment, you are basking in it. Focus your attention in your magical surrounds and add as many details as you can, such as: people, feelings, and senses, to create a bigger momentum to your story. See yourself as the main character and be your own director.

What do you see? What are you doing in this moment? Is it day or night? What season? Is it cold? Are you indoors or outdoors? How do you feel now that you experience your desire? Are there other people with you? Where do you stand? How do others respond to you? Now, what more do you want to achieve?

Think outside the box and let your mind wonder in beautiful ideas. Remember that your desire is available to you and there is no such thing as limitation for all is energy that can be attracted. You hold the magnet now in your hand. Attract it your way. Describe to us how it makes you feel. Speak of it out loud or in your mind so we can always hear you. Tell us why you want this. How would it change your life? What areas of your life are to be affected? Does it assist others as well? If it is here *now*, what would it bring alongside with it, what other emotions? Freedom, joy, well-being?

Ultimately, you may not experience the exact image you create, but you will achieve the same emotion. Set your story and add details to create a stronger feeling, for that feeling is to be translated from the cosmos, and be brought back to you. Make those high energy emotions work for you. Be in this quiet and joy as many times as you want. Imagine, and create your future environment. Remember, we and the cosmos watch and understand through emotions and energy. Focus on all that you experience in your imagination, and those energies will become stronger, and add momentum to your story. As your story expands in your mind, so will your emotions, as well as the expansion of your desires.

This technique, should not feel as a burden, on the contrary, it should be fun and uplifting. If you feel you must do it to get to where you want to be, it will not work. Be in that moment because you want to bask in that emotion, because it excites you and brings you bliss; because in that moment, you no longer desire anything, for you have it all already.

Adding emotions from experiences lived before, can be another method to bring forth a strong emotion. Recall details from a memory that caused you to relive that desirable feeling, so you can bask in it longer. For instance if you want to attract a new partner, remember how excited and loved you felt in previous experiences. Stay in that feeling and add new images and settings. Likewise, how did you feel last time you earned a lot of money? Remember the excitement as you counted them? As you recall the feeling, the experiences come to match the frequency.

It is really as simple as that; there is nothing hard for you to do, nor a task to follow every day. Attend to your imagination every time you are in need of feeling good. Have fun with it and enjoy the results; use it to bring beautiful experiences in your life. Bask in the glory of what you want, invite it in your now, find the feeling, pretend it to life and bring your wishes to materialization.

We feel through your emotions.

CHAPTER 45

ACHIEVE AN ABUDANT MINDSET

Nothing is unattainable since all are energy. For this, all events and circumstances can be available to you if you summon, and allow their energy to join you. A large sum of money, a penny, a partner, a house, all are first nothing but energy. Summon that energy, and allow it as it comes. On this note, we bring you a method that you can use to summon forth the energy of your desires, but for it to work, you mustn't contradict it.

Nothing is set in stone; events and circumstances change according to your own responses. If you allow several minutes a day to imagine your desire, but your everyday behavior contradicts it, you block it from arriving. Let's assume you desire a new car, you gone through all the steps to materialize it, and you imagine it in your possession everyday. However, you constantly complain about how inconvenient it is to live without a vehicle, and so your are mixed up from positive to negative and you do not allow your desire to manifest. The more you attend to your thoughts, the more alert you become as to what energy you vibrate, and hence, the more power you have to remove or shift energy to match you. Use it wisely.

Sit in a quiet place for several moments with the intention of summoning energy in your being. Hold the intention that all the energy you will summon, is to assist you bring *financial abundance* — or anything else you desire. See yourself increasing in power and focus. Imagine big, white, energetic fields around you. Embrace their power for a while and do not fear; it is but an energy that comes and goes by the attention you give to it; if you focus on it, it expands. Talk to it now, instruct it. Ask it to summon forth anything that you desire. Instruct it in this way:

"I am now ready to receive the flow of abundance for this certain desire to now enter my life. I lay in acknowledgment that you will move circumstances and events to bring it to me when the time is right. I lovingly ask you Energy, to assist this event to enter my life experience easily and effortlessly. Allow the cosmos to bring it to me as described, or bring me something better. I dearly thank you. It is for my best well-being and for the greatest and highest good of all."

Now feel the energy expand from around you. Imagine the event you wish to bring forth. Imagine yourself holding it, purchasing an object with it, counting it. Feel the happiness it brings you. Do this, to direct all that energy to bring you that matter in physical reality. And now, see the energy move and disappear. It works to bring that feeling back to you.

Words do not matter unless they are accompanied with focused attention or emotion. You need to see it with your mind's eye, feel it from within your being, and then it will be so.

THE TRUTH OF ALL THAT IS

Following, see a golden energy surrounding you. This is the energy of your desire that has joined your own aura. It empowers you, brings you confidence. Your desire is there, energetically, waiting the right moment to manifest in the physical. Enjoy its frequency; it is yours. It will stay for as long as you desire, believe it, and allow it in your experience.

Be aware to not contradict those energies. Stop complaining about your income and desire; shift the story into a positive one for you. Instead of *"I do not have enough for what I need"* say *"my needs are being taken care of, and I know there is more underway."* With these simple words, you allow it to materialize.

Rest assured that the energy you have summoned has been captured, has been given momentum, and is truly there to fulfill its task. Feel the force of the energy surrounding you.

Feel free to repeat the ritual when needed, but do not attend to it too often, as that is a sign of poor belief of its materialization. Let the universe work its magic; believe that it is now done and let it go.

There are no limitations to the cosmos.

Let the flow of abundance shine upon you.

CHAPTER 46

GO WITH THE FLOW

When you control your thoughts, you limit unwanted experiences from entering your life. Allow the events and circumstance to appear, acknowledge and appreciate them to allow your desires to flow into your experience.

You have created your wish list with all the desires you want to have. You understand that nothing is too big for the universe to bring, and most importantly, that you are worthy of happiness. In this way, you allow. You go about your days not worrying, not wondering nor doubting whether your desire will appear, or when, or how. You do not force it; you do not try to make it happen. You do not visualize or make lists or affirm in order for it to appear, but enjoy the feeling, and have fun. You just trust that when it is time, it will arrive. Bask in happiness, and allow the universe to bring your desires in perfect time and way.

If you recognize that one thing does not serve you, and you shout "No!" at it, you go against your desirable outcome.

"*No, I do not want to receive more bills,*" "*No, I do not accept that I am without a job,*" "*No, I can't believe that this person broke up with me. No, no, no!*" But the universe only receives attention. Positive or negative, yes or no, the universe only receives "Yes." And so, our physical friends, if you resist at a certain event, you include it in your experience. Let it pass you by with no effect, but shift it into a positive experience. Why do you worry that a person broke up with you? Do you wish to limit yourself to a person that does not appreciate you enough? Old leaves for new to appear. This is a way for the cosmos to bring you change. If one does the same things over and over, thinks the same thoughts, sees the same people, does the same tasks, then they do not evolve. They do not bring themselves positive changes; they stay the same. You are not to stay the same, you are to enjoy and appreciate and love and experience. Go with the flow; all are lessons to learn but your attitude is all that makes them so. Accept and do not resist them, so they stop repeating. See them as good, and so they shall be, deny them, and they will create more displeasure.

The law of creating and allowing is the same for all matters. You cannot stop an experience from entering into your life, but you can alter it to serve you. Live, enjoy your lifetime, create beautiful experiences and allow them in your physical reality. If you are too busy shouting "No" at them, you resist your desires. Everything is a blessing; see it as such, and you make way for many more true blessings to arise. The world is filled with your energies; use them wisely. You are on the right path. You are doing alright.

All is well. You are flowing.

CHAPTER 47

PREPARE FOR ARRIVAL

Instead of worrying and pushing your desires further away; you must enjoy the process of creating. If any action brings you worry, fear or distress the result will not be beneficial. The same way, if waiting for your desire is making you impatient, then you are not allowing it. In this chapter, we assist you with the final process of allowing your desires to manifest.

When you get impatient waiting for a desire, you worry and doubt whether it will materialize. You do not trust the universe, but signal it with negative energies as to how things are not working out. They are working out. *You are going to receive your desires in your physical reality.* These processes we present here, will give you a peace of mind.

No matter if you have affirmed, visualized, prayed or pretended to manifest your desires, all methods are equally effective and have indeed created your desire. You have established a link with the final outcome, and added it enough momentum to materialize. No matter if you have done this for an hour, a day, weeks or months, it is done. From this point on, there is nothing else for you to do. If you keep adding to it, you block it by trying too hard. Once you have set a belief that it is happening, you are satisfied with what you have created, and the thought of it makes you happy, then it is time to step away from the process and make way for manifestation.

To prepare for its arrival, let go of the struggle, and know it is as finished. It is quite similar to a family expecting eagerly a new baby. They know it is coming and they prepare for the arrival. They do not overstress when or how it will come. They know that the baby will arrive when it is time, and they patiently expect it. In the meantime, the family prepares a room for the baby, buys clothes for it, a bed and even toys; you are advised to do the same. Make way in your life to receive it. Do you expect your new partner? Clear a drawer for them; sleep on one side of the bed to leave them space. A new car, perhaps? Do you have space to store it? Create a covered, secure area. You want a certain amount of money, perhaps. What would you do once the money is there? Make a plan on how you will invest it. How would you keep it safe? Prepare the territory for this new change that is coming into your life. In this way, you also prepare for it emotionally. Make yourself, your family and your area ready for arrival. Your desires are in the process of materializing; the baby is coming to life. Are you ready to receive?

Let go of worry and neediness and know it is actually *done*. Prepare; it is about to come to life.

Get ready.

PART IV: EMPOWEREMENT

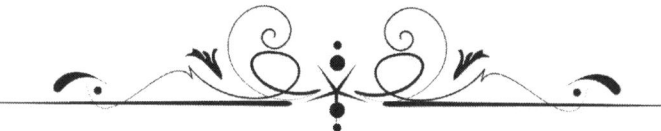

CHAPTER 48

ASK FOR A SIGN

We are in awe of your wit, of your ability to control your reality, of the pureness you hold in your heart. All of you, are so magnificent, even if you do not realize it; we see your beauty, we know your power. You are unlimited like us, and it is time to really see it so.

We have been telling you over and over and we will continue to until you believe us. You see, if you do not think it is possible or that you are worthy, how can you go about creating beautiful things for yourself? This is where your power lies and your awakening begins. Many of you want proof in order to believe, faith not on words spoken but on acts that are seen. We understand it so, and sometimes we bring it to you, but you cannot really see. The things you cannot comprehend, you deny, even if proof is in front of your very eyes. You call events "coincidences," as if there is such thing as random. Nothing is. All have their purpose. You are here in an order, as everything is chosen in detail. All people and events that come into your path are so beautifully set out for a higher purpose. Divine Timing is not a coincidence either. It is God's way of bringing about affairs together that are aligned with each other. And so, there is a reason for all, yet you really want more to see, to believe of your power, of what we are telling you to be true. So ask us.

Pick a sign, something you are not resistant to at first. Something that once it is brought into your awareness, you will really know that all we have been telling you are true. Close your eyes and invoke us with a simple sentence:
"Angels of the Light, I call upon you now to bring my awareness on such item or matter, to help me really see, really believe. I am ready to awaken. Open my eyes to the truth. And so it is."

Now picture something you wish to see, or even hear. A feather, unicorns, a ship's horn, child's laughter, a song, numbers. Picture it so we know what it is and bring it to you. The signs you choose can be anything; simply give your slight awareness on them, and so they shall be.

Once you receive what you have asked for, there is nothing else for you to doubt. Open your heart to the Angels and to this book, and really embrace this knowledge. It is your time to shine, to uncover your power, to know your potential. You have asked us for all of these and now we respond. We bring to you if you ask; you create if you believe.

Go about your day, knowing that your sign will appear, if not ask again with a mind - not occupied by thought; it will arrive, for we are always around, know, and always respond. Believe us, experience your capabilities, understand the truth, find your power; awaken.

You are magnificent.

CHAPTER 49

THE SIGNIFICANCE OF YOUR THOUGHTS

Sometimes, as you contemplate, your focus wanders in different matters. Thoughts come in many forms, and while some should not be given any attention, others occur to enlighten, or offer assistance.

Blockages come about in the form of repeated thoughts, in order to be acknowledged and removed. If you hold your attention towards them for a long period of time, they continue to reside in your subconscious. For instance if you think of a negative event that occurred a while ago, do you let it in? It probably makes its way to the surface in order to be released from your experience and memory because it does not serve you any longer. Once it is released, it cannot affect you, it will be deleted. Let it pass your awareness and be on its way. All thoughts big or small, wondrous or not, try to get your attention, but you must choose which ones to allow in, and which ones to let go of.

Thoughts may also occur because someone else linked you to an event or idea with their thought. In that case, you picked up their frequency. This is common with people you have a close link with; you think of them, and the phone rings with them on the other line.

What is more, thoughts may occur to bring you a message from us. In this case, the thought is more firm and lightened. Ideas and inspiration come to you in this way, to bring assistance.

Also, thoughts may bring a message from other spiritual beings that were once your physical family or friends. These souls try to get your attention to bring you their messages and let you know they are alright. If something reminds you of them, they have triggered your thoughts. Acknowledge them and do not be afraid; they want to let you know that all is well.

Another form of thought comes about from your own Higher Self trying to bring you a lesson or assurance. If you get a positive thought associated with uplifting energy, you are aligned with your Higher Self that assures you that thought is positive. For instance, if you contemplate upon going somewhere and you receive a positive emotion within you, your Higher Self is in agreement, and that is something that you must consider, as it will be beneficial.

If a thought occurs that you did not turn off the cooker, is it one that should get your attention? Thoughts that come on stronger and force your attention to strike are possibly a message from us or your Higher Self giving you a warning.

Contemplation helps you bring to the surface unwanted matters, clear your mind from worries, bring you messages or to give you warnings. On the same note, it is alright to speak to yourself, it helps you clarify thoughts, receive inspiration and ideas, it brings clarity. If it helps, we are listening.

Attend to your thoughts and let them wonder regularly; clear your mind from the unwanted ones, and make way for the positive. Any thought that comes to the surface, is doing so for a reason. Keep them or let them go.

We speak to you through your thoughts.

CHAPTER 50

YOUR EVERYDAY INTERACTIONS

Often, when a person is new to you, you tend to judge them and fill your energies with negative responses towards them. Then the interactions become challenging and cause unbalanced relationships. Responses and characters vary, but everyone is the same in energy. You are all family and created by equal, focused attention.

No one said you should like everyone, but judgment and gossip sends negative vibrations to both you and the person of your attention. On the other hand, when you speak loving and kind words about another, both parts benefit. Your tone sets out energies that break into the cosmos, along with any other thought you attend to. If you gossip on a regular basis, limit it and you will feel better.

Common interactions among strangers are not easy for most of you, since you feel uncomfortable and awkward for this unknown person staring back at you. It is okay to know that this person is very similar to you; you might even be from the same spirit family, have common Spirit Guides that brought you together, have a common cause, or perhaps you knew them well in another lifetime. All these are quite common, and sometimes your Spirit Guides decide it is a good idea to bring you two together believing you will benefit from each other. Ultimately, they may become a good friend, a partner, a person who is going to offer you a job, a reference that is going to serve you, or even give you advice. Do not hurry to judge someone by the looks or character, because then you close the link of connection with them, and thus any benefits you could have gotten from that interaction. Have an open mind against all others and trust that all is for your highest good.

You now realize that ideas, people and events do not come randomly, but that they are there to offer you something valuable. Welcome all opportunities and people with joy and keep something positive from all experiences. Your Spirit Guides always work to assist you, and the cosmos brings forth what you have asked for; in that regard, anything can be of value, and so do not be so quick to dismiss it. Something someone tells you may even be your next step to take towards your goals and desires, or a warning from us. If you dislike that person, you will not receive the message. Give it a chance; maybe someone or something, somehow will be that thing you have been waiting for.

Lay alert at all times, as any opportunity can come from various resources, and many are in disguise. Gossip and judgment restrain you from beneficial interactions. See the good in all that exists, and remember that all of you are creations of God and have a right to be just as you are. Color, ethnicity, age, appearance–, nothing matters as God only sees the soul. Come together co-existing and benefit from one another.

You have so much to give to each other.

CHAPTER 51

DIVINE OPPORTUNITIES

There are endless opportunities every day, a variety of paths to choose from and people to interact with. There are no right or wrong choices, there are only different life paths with different lessons and experiences.

Left or right, yes or no, go or not. Every day you face a plethora of options that the universe has created for you. Some of them are there to give experiences, others to respond to your own thoughts and desires. You face them every day, consciously or unconsciously. Every choice you make creates your present and future. There are no predestined paths; you choose according to your free will. Sometimes, you choose the ones that feel good; you go with your inspiration, you act towards how you feel. Other times, you go against what you believe, what you want, what you really wish. Why is that? Live by your truth and do not hesitate to take an opportunity, love and have fun. Those experiences and pleasures are there for you; the resources of the cosmos never run out. There are times, you follow another's path and beliefs. If one likes a path or has a certain belief, that does not mean all benefit from it. Find your own truth, walk your own path.

Why do you do the same things you have done for years, surround yourself with the same people, or make the same choices? If something does not please you, change it. Change is a way to evolve. God is fond of change and believes that all should move forth. Do not be afraid to start something new, a hobby, a job. If done with an open heart, it will be a blessed change for you. If you have something in your mind recently but did not get to do; do it now. This is your sign to move forward. Change can be anything; a change in your schedule brings new energy in your life. Embrace it. Your life's path expands and unfolds with every decision you make, any road you choose and any event that appears. Remember: staying in one place cannot offer you anything new nor it helps you to grow.

Do not be afraid to act. Inspiration is an impulse to act upon your gut, to do something new, to take a new road, a new opportunity, to make a change, act by inspiration and you will create miracles. Let go of your fears of the unknown, trust that there is something better for you ahead. The world is filled with endless opportunities; be optimistic and you shall find your way.

Does a new opportunity or idea light you up? Then follow it; do not be afraid to fail, as that cannot be. If one does not succeed in the way they hoped, but acted on inspiration and bliss, they cannot loose. Opportunities make their way to you all the time; choose them. The world's endless abundance lies in front of you. Follow the trails from within; you will get there in time.

You are surrounded by love.

CHAPTER 52

ALLOW DIVINE ENERGY WITHIN

There is nothing in this world that you cannot be, do or have. You hold the power for all the gifts you wish, to enter into your experience. Take pride of your accomplishments and bask in the beauty of what there is to come. A bright future awaits you.

The time is now to expand you, and shift your energies to match who you really are. Close your eyes and bring your awareness in the space on and above your forehead. Stay still and bask in all those emotions rising up within you. Take long deep breaths and feel the energy of the cosmos entering your being. You will soon bask in deeper appreciation and feel more energetic and joyful. Enjoy in the beauty of what surrounds you, feel your power, sense the Divine Connection in you, now.

Right this moment, we reside within your being. We are there, sending you positive vibrations. Feel them, sense them, bask in them. We open doors for you, we make way for many beautiful things to enter your experience. We connect you with your true self; allow us.

See with your closed eyes a source of Light shining through you in the space right above your head. You invite Divine energies like this and as you do, you feel uplifting energy and well-being.

Bask in moments like these for several minutes, as often as you can, and it should be enough for you to expand; to remove layers of negativity that keep you grounded and stuck, to remove resistance. Then, as you acknowledge the presence of Divine Power radiating within you and to you, your life will shift towards more positive experiences and more well-being.

Little by little, you will feel more and more Divine Energies. It is alright if you cannot feel all that different from your first attempt; it will get better, and when it does, you will too; you will soon feel stronger, more energized.

There is a glorious life that awaits you now, as you stay positive, as you take several moments to feel your energies rise, as you allow Divine Light to grow in your being, you will become awaken and more alert.

Take several moments each day with this exercise to absorb Divine Energies. Do not fear if you hear us talk from within your being. We simply let you know how well you are doing and how proud we are of you. You may even see us with your closed eyes. All is well; bask in the beauty of the Light, in the serenity of Mother Nature.

> We are empowering you now.

CHAPTER 53

CLEAR YOUR THOUGHTS AND BE HAPPY NOW

Each second, your mind holds many different thoughts with various frequencies; these various thoughts exhaust you mentally, and affect your responses and experiences. Clear those old thoughts to release old negative vibrations; so that, you clear your energy and prevent their negative frequencies to enter your next thought or activity.

It does not take more than a minute, but the advantages of the following exercise are plenty.

Take a moment in silence and breathe deeply in and out, and let go of any thoughts. Concentrate only on your breathing. As you focus on this process, your mind clears up and lets go of thoughts that lie in your awareness. Do this technique regularly, because energies easily transmit from one person to the other, from one thought to another.

Clearing your awareness centers your focus and welcomes

positive frequencies within. You are beings of energy, and your attention is needed in each task to perform well. Either learning something new or succeeding in a project, attention is a requirement. But what happens when you move your attention from a thought like: *"I am not feeling well"* to writing a letter? The letter is messy, and the final result is not pleasing. This is due to your negative frequency being transmitted to your new task, which acquires a similar frequency. If you take a moment to clear the previous thought and its energy, your letter will turn out more satisfying.

When you wake up in the morning, you start anew; you hold no resistance and no negative energies in your being. The same happens if you are happy. However, if you went to sleep sad, then once you wake up, you recall that frequency and you return to that state. As you go about your day, you keep transmitting the same energy from task to task, thought to thought. So take a moment and breathe, clear your mind and then begin something new.

Your mind is filled with thoughts *I should do this and that, clean, shop, prepare dinner, pay the bills, take the kids to practice*. There are always things to attend to, but as you focus on these tasks, your life is drained and you do not have time to really live and enjoy the beauty that surrounds you. You came on Earth eagerly, anticipating great experiences and a life well lived. Once you leave this world, your soul lusts to be satisfied, filled with joy and love and beautiful memories. Awaken into all that exists in your life and not only the things needed to be done, or be acquired. You have so many already.

Happiness is your true state of being. Happiness circulates energy in and out of your body, from you and to you. The road to happiness has neither laws nor predestined paths; it is a choice you follow. Notice and count all that you make you happy now, and appreciate them. Acknowledge something pleasing when it arrives to invite more like it in your life. Love all, act in kindness, spent time with people and activities you love and enjoy; all of those are ways to bring happiness in your present moment, and clear away old troubles.

The key to a happy state of mind, relies on your emotions in the present. To enjoy the present, clear the old thoughts, and appreciate what surrounds you and enjoy it. Let's give you an example so you get the hang of it. How is it that your legs rest on that chair? How does it make you feel? How beautiful it is that your back is supported? Are you outside? Is the wind caressing your skin? Do you breath in the oxygen, smell the flowers, listen to the wind blowing within the trees? Or are you inside basking in warmth and quiet? How amazing is it, that you are surrounded by many of your loving things? They bring you joy and peace, don't they? Are you enjoying the words of this book? How does it make you feel? Do you feel uplifted, rejoiced, in control? All of these emotions exist in this moment, you see. Your present is filled with joyful emotions that are overseen as you rush about your life worrying about what is next. This is your *now*, and this is all that is at this moment; make the best of it.

If you are not satisfied with one situation, change it. Radiate joy and happiness so it becomes fulfilling and brightens your life. Who said tasks such as cleaning or homework should be unsatisfying? Associate them with something you love, and they will then gain some of those positive energies. For instance, listen to your favorite music or dance while cleaning, or pet your kitten while studying. Like this, you ensure a pleasurable outcome and your energies are uplifted anytime you start upon those tasks again. Life should be fun, so make it so.

Your present is the most powerful moment you will ever

have. Bask in the now; be at ease, appreciative and joyful. Whenever you are stressed or troubled, take it as a sign to follow the above technique, to bring calm back in your being. Notice what is in your present, and do not worry about what is next. From a state of calmness and joy, reassure yourself that it is going to turn out all right, and so it shall be. As you begin to practice this some more, you invite in your life many uplifting experiences. The more you bask in the moment, the more your near future becomes peaceful and joyful. This is the key to expanding yourself, live without negative thoughts, and enjoy your life.

Allow several moments every day to pause, breathe and enjoy the moment, to clear the negative energies to ensure a healthy flow of positive energy and good mood.

Pause and breathe.

CHAPTER 54

RETURN TO PURITY

When you were a baby, you knew that your life will be filled with joy and you were eager to learn and expand. You came from purity and still hold pure Divine Energies. Growing up, this anticipation and eagerness for joy and love are replaced with limitations, boundaries, hate and wrong perceptions given by those around you. In this chapter, we reveal several practices to assist you to bring the Light back into your life.

For the energies to flow in and out of your life, you must give out the same way you receive. The simplest form of this energetic exchange, is with material things. You know how beautiful it is to be given something new. When it enters into your experience, it brings you joy. Remember when you were a kid and someone gave you a new toy? This is the beautiful feeling of joy from receiving. It is quite fulfilling, and appears regularly through many forms in your experience; either by a new partner, a loving friend, an item, a car, a child, a pet or even the return of a lost item. Bask in the energy of having something new. Feel how beautiful this feeling makes you, how true you feel at that moment.

Similarly, giving to the world holds good vibrations since you spread joy to someone else. The feeling is mutual, and can be transferred from receiver to the giver, and thus it benefits both. Sharing an item with another or giving when you have plenty holds the feeling of pride, worthiness, good deed and love. Giving has a double effect; one from your own satisfaction from spreading joy, and secondly from the response of the receiver that shares their feelings and energy back to you. Also, the cosmos receives the frequency of all those pure energies, captures them and later brings them back to the giver, multiplied. In that regard, giving or receiving holds pure intentions and continues the flow of natural pure energy. And so, share with others anything that you can spare, whether it's material things, assistance or attention.

Another way to restore your energy is to spend more time in nature that holds pure, Divine vibrations. Spend more time around flowers, plants and animals as you capture some of their Divine Energy within. Breathe often for fresh oxygen to bring in pure energy. Similarly, drink a lot of water, as it holds pureness from nature. Bathe in the sea or a lake to purify your being. Bask in the sun, or watch the moon and the stars to invite Divine Energy from the cosmos. Air and water, basking in nature, and spending time with animals assures uplifting energy and well-being.

Another beneficial practice is prayer. When you pray, you let go of troubles and trust Divine energies for help. In this way, you invite pure energy in your life as well as release worry and fear. Go on, talk to us; we are always here for you and always listen.

Meditate, color, spend time alone to put your thoughts in order and clear your mind from troubles. Quieting your mind from troubles and thoughts, allows your Higher Self to guide you.

Be in the moment; notice what happens around you, as this will ground you in the present. Relax and smell the flowers, appreciate all sounds, count your blessings, love where you stand.

Be around people you love, spent time in their presence. Uplifting people in combination with fun moments of joy and serenity with those you love, are truly a powerful experience you should attend to regularly. You have chosen these people to enter your life even before reincarnation for a reason, so go on: plan a game night with your children, go out to have fun with your family and friends, go for a walk with your partner. Be released from negative thoughts to have a fun time, it will surely be a time to remember.

Let go of the hate and resentment that you hold for people who have wronged you. This is the time to contemplate upon those and forgive. Forgiveness is an amazing occurrence, because it holds so much good energy, and clears away bad negativity from your being. Do not do it for them, do it for you. Sit in quiet and make peace with those you hold resentment towards. You can even write them a letter -- you don't have to send it, but it can clear your thoughts and focus. Tell them in your letter how much they have wronged you with their ways, but also, that you understand their part as well. Reason with them through your words, and ultimately forgive them. Your faith will be restored; you would have released negative thoughts from within. All is truly well, my loving friends. You came here to be pure and holding resentment for another does not harm anyone but you. Let it go and return to purity.

There are more ways to uplift your being that may work different for each one. Find the ones you love the most and attend to them often. We believe in you.

Restore your being. It is time.

CHAPTER 55

REWRITE OR DELETE

We explained how important a joyful state of being is, as high frequencies result to well-being. Further we present two simple techniques to take control of all interactions and events to keep you in high vibrations.

If an unwelcome person crosses your path that brings you trouble and lower energy, each time you face them, you instantly radiate negative emotions. If, you find something positive from your interaction with them, every time you see them your energies shift. With repetition and attention given to positive aspects; the negative emotions will be replaced, and only bring you positive emotions. This technique, needs some getting used to, especially if you really dislike a person or circumstance. Know, that each time you attend to that thought and try to shift it, a piece of that negative puzzle is erased and replaced with a positive one. In time the puzzle will be completed with only positive pieces, that bring you satisfaction and good energy.

Another method to keep your energy intact, is to avoid that person or experience all together. This way you prevent negative energies to enter your attention, and so their responses will have no effect on you. However, by avoiding them, they will never be shifted or removed, but continue to affect you once they are given attention.

Note anything that is bothering you and brings about negative emotions. Be determined to shift a belief so that it does not affect your positive attitude. For example, if you wrote *"a bill is arriving"* on your list, then you have created certain negative connotations towards this experience, and every time you receive a bill, bad emotions rise up and take control of your energies. Since you cannot avoid the action altogether, you must alter its energies. Cross that sentence off and replace it with. *"I love receiving bills,"* and then state why. Why do you love it? Perhaps you have received services that you are satisfied with. Without these kinds of services, you wouldn't have electricity, nor cable, nor water. Those are truly magical blessings and paying the bill is simply your kind acknowledgment towards them, and your way to say *"Thank you."*

So, say: *"Thank you and I love how you work, so that I am given all these beautiful experiences and utilities. And so I love paying my bills!"* In this way, you stated how grateful you are for that bill, and you have replaced the negative connotations with new ones. Any time you have to pay a bill now, replace your thoughts with these new ones, to continue the positive flow of abundance.

These two techniques are important to assist you in creating a life full of joy and peace. Set their tone right, or avoid them altogether. Do not endure negative thoughts in your life because you always deserve to have high vibrations. Acknowledge, take control, and rewrite or delete anything that bothers you.

You deserve to be happy.

CHAPTER 56

EVERYDAY TECHNIQUES

Have you heard of the saying "whatever you sow you shall reap?" Your responses and thoughts let you reap the rewards as the universe responds back to you, with equivalent events. In this chapter, we bring a new perspective into your everyday life. Follow our guidance and you shall reap the rewards.

Before you begin something new, take a deep breath beforehand, clear your mind and state: *"This is going to turn out beautifully."* Whatever that activity is – baking a cake, a new painting, a drive in your car, or even going grocery shopping – you direct the result. In this way, you bring forth fulfilling energies that allow you to release contradicting ones, and so the universe knows; and so it shall be.

On the same note, begin your day with positive thoughts. As soon as you wake up; smile to the universe, realize what a beautiful night sleep you had, how rested you feel, and then say in your mind or out loud: *"I cannot wait to see what the universe has in store for me today! Make this an exciting, fun day! And so it is!"* and up you go. From early in the day, you bring a new attitude and high frequency, so the universe cannot but follow your positive vibrations.

Whenever something happens that pleases you, acknowledge it and praise the universe for it. Like a teacher praising a student, praise the moment you just had. If you had a wonderful meal, say in your mind or out loud: *"I loved this, thank you."* And so, the universe will bring you more like it. Be aware not to use this the other way around. For example, when you say "I don't like this," you activate negative attention. For this, only focus on your beautiful, satisfying experiences.

Bless those around you; spread positivity and uplifting energy. As you focus on giving blessings to others, you invite more to join you. Acknowledge the good work of another, the good services you just received, or even the satisfying technology that you used. Acknowledge those positive aspects to spread positive energy. And so, bless anyone you meet and say thank you. Blessing others is like blessing yourself.

Is that mailman happy today? Perhaps he could use an uplifting energy. Just smile to them; it transmits positive energy. The receiver cannot do anything but smile back to you, and the exchange offers uplifting energy to both parts. Moreover, those who offer a true smile hold no resistance in their being at that moment.

Laughter, is even more uplifting than a smile, but you know this already, as you have tried it several times. When you laugh, you cannot be resistant; at that moment you only hold the amusing event in your focus, and everything else falls away and disappears.

A good laugh several times makes you vibrate on fast frequencies that have amazing responses from the universe. Go on, try laughing often; it will genuinely loosen your negative vibrations and increase your positivity flow. Being too serious never served anyone.

In that regard, it is worthy to mention tears. Some hold the idea that crying is equivalent to sadness. The truth is that tears are a response of the being to release it. Do not hold tears in; let them flow; you will feel much better.

Here is another easy technique to bring you back to a happy state if you are in misalignment: All of you have people or circumstances that you enjoy more than others; think of one that causes you to be the most grateful. Perhaps a child, a job, a memory, a lover or even a compliment or an experience. Those, when recalled, bring about only pure, positive emotions to you, since they are those who have the most positive impact on your energy. The more you attend to these people, memories, events or circumstances, with your thought, the more lighted your aura becomes, and the more enjoyable your life experience gets. And so, whenever you are in misalignment, recall whatever makes you happy, and focus on the way it makes you feel. For instance, your child: you are proud of the person they have become, you love them so, you are grateful that God has blessed you with such a magnificent offspring. Keep adding until you feel elevated, until you feel deep appreciation and peace.

If in misalignment, recall any event or circumstance that is most pleasing to you and add more momentum until your negative emotions are replaced with joy. The more you practice it, the more you become accustomed to the feeling that person, thought or event brings to you, and so it is easier to recall it. Have several blessings hidden up your sleeve and use them when in need of high frequencies.

Remember, the happier you are the more blessings you bring in your life. Laugh more, smile more, always be positive and enjoy the moment.

Did you smile yet?

CHAPTER 57

SHIELD YOURSELF

Take time to be alone and love who you are, this is the only way you can create miracles. Being alone is valuable, since you can clear your energy, set your goals, pray, meditate, write your thoughts on paper and bask in the moment to invite positive energy, accomplish your goals, and create a life full of beauty. You do not need anyone else to make you feel good, for you must learn to enjoy your own company more than anyone else's, so that you are not be affected by others' perceptions. Use the techniques we describe below to restore your energy, center your being, and shield yourself.

There are those times you feel overwhelmed when around people. Your surroundings easily become stressful and drain your energy. If you are in a crowded place, your attention can easily be directed anywhere, and this drains your energy, you feel dizzy, get a headache or even asthma and perhaps feel exhausted. Those are signs it is time to step away from the crowd. Do not worry if that occurs; it is but a confirmation that your energy requires more attention, because you infuse negative ones from your surroundings. This is called empathy and you have this ability naturally within.

Empathy is a way non-physical beings communicate; we read each other's frequencies. For you, it is indeed, a blessing, but requires caution with interactions. See it as a confirmation that you have mastered a deeper connection with yourself and your natural state of being, that you reject the negative frequencies of others. Think of it like the stronger affect the weaker. Good energy spreads as you enter a room full of people that are less positive than you. When you interact with them, you naturally pass on your energy, and so you are left more drained when there's a big crowd. To restore your focus and energy, you must be alone in quiet for a while. Contemplate or focus on your breathing to re-center your focus. When you do, you will be more energetic and positive.

The more time you spend alone, the more you get use to serenity and energy, that you become overwhelmed when surrounded by others. At this time, we will ask you to take a note of anything or anyone that causes your energies to drain, and try to avoid them or avoid that place or attend that task, at least before restoring your energy and shielding yourself.

We present a simple technique you can use to protect yourself from absorbing unwelcomed energies from others. Close your eyes and imagine a white, bright Light surrounding you. It is the form of your energy that lies in your aura. Just imagine it shinning, feel its Light within. Embrace it's warmth for several seconds and then say:

"My powerful shining Light, I ask that you are protected by unwelcomed negative energies of others. Shield and rest your power with the help of several

Lighted Angels. Merge your shine with mine, save me from any darkness and negativity. And so it is."

This prayer invites Divine Energies to shield and protect you. Repetition is required as the shield fades in time. Protect your energy regularly to keep it intact.

Whenever you are in need of positive energies we are always a call away to restore them. Remember, the more powerful you become, the more you will feel empowered and cheerful. Empathy is but a way to understand vibrational frequencies. As you become more positive, you will attract people and events with similar vibrations. Treasure your energies and do not allow others to limit them.

You are stronger that way.

CHAPTER 58

CROWN CHAKRA

You must find your Light that hides all your power; unravel it, use it for good. For this, we present the ways you can communicate with your divinity. Crown chakra is a portal of connection with your non-physical self that guides you in all you want to achieve.

The more you align with your Higher Self, the more power you hold. To connect with your higher self, you must take control of your emotions and guide your thoughts. In the crown chakra, lies your spiritual cord that is your connection with spirit. If you attend to it regularly and clear the negative vibrations, it renews and straightens you as a whole, spiritually and physically. If it is cleared, it can move energy to you for well-being, and to your thoughts so they are added enough momentum for materialization. This way you allow your positive thoughts to materialize in a faster rate.

Try this exercise now. Close your eyes and remain in quiet. Focus on the area above your head, your "crown chakra" as many call it. The crown chakra is the portal of communication between the physical and non-physical world, between you and us, you and the universe. Focus on that area now with the intention to heighten and unblock it. Remove any thoughts, feel white light radiating to that area and empowering it. You may experience strong, positive emotions; you may sense a tingling sensation on your forehead or above your head. Do not get alarmed; it is the energy moving, your chakra opening wider. Breathe slowly with focus on that chakra, when you have gained enough higher energy you will be uplifted, lighter, happier, healthier.

With this simple exercise, you empower your spiritual cord, and you infuse with pure energy. This crown chakra holds your spiritual connection. If you put your focus on it, you feel the energy move through your whole being. With attention, you enhance it so you can receive Divine assistance and inspiration more easily, and be more aware of your surroundings. As your crown chakra clears, you will feel extended, unique, powerful. Even if you have never meditated, you will sense the shift of energies as they move through you. You will become aware, alert, expand and purify. Welcome the energies within; you are but a being with so much strength; uncover your potential, sense your energy.

Feel your power expand you.

CHAPTER 59

CONNECTING WITH YOUR HIGHER SELF

Your Higher Self is a part of you already, but you can tune in to its spiritual power and receive universal assistance directly. The non-physical part of you brings you enlightenment, purpose, and inspiration, and completes your existence. Connecting your two parts will only bring you more energy, wisdom and assistance. We show you the way to a direct connection.

You already connected with your Higher Self several times already, but you are not aware of it. Interactions like that are hard to distinguish, because they are too close to your own thoughts; there is a reason this is so. Imagine you heard an external thought giving you advices and guidance. You would feel scared, overwhelmed and probably refuse the advice. So, a communication occurs internally in your mind that forms thoughts that bring you guidance. An example of Higher Self communication is when you get inspiration or a creative solution to a problem. Thoughts given by your Higher Self are always wise, positive and uplifting.

You are ready for a direct communication with your Higher Self, since we have given you a basic understanding of what there is to know, and we have helped you open up to infinite wisdom. Now you can connect and receive communication directly, to find all that you are still doubting.

This technique is called "automatic writing" or "flow of consciousness writing," to connect consciously with your Higher Self; continue without caution.

Sit in quiet with a piece of paper and pen in front of you. Close your eyes, clear you thoughts, and release any expectations or fear. Take a few breaths and write:

"Higher Self, please connect with me now in this way, and offer me a reassuring thought that you are with me."

Give it some time; a thought will appear in your mind. Do not judge it, fear or over-think it. Whatever comes, write it down. If you feel you made it up, it is alright keep writing the thoughts that come, and you will soon be able to differentiate your own thoughts from any higher wisdom. Your Higher Self always connects with you, but it is a matter of how much you allow it to come through. Usually, with their response, they will give you welcoming message of love and support. As you distance your own thoughts and emotions, you will notice the responses become associated with strong, loving emotions.

If you cannot concentrate or receive any divine thoughts, meditate first and try again.

The same way you started a conversation with your infinite wisdom, ask for a message, or anything that you need assistance with. Write all thoughts down without pausing to consider them;

neither judge them; you can pause after you finish the conversation.

Naturally, the thoughts will begin to flow like flashes in your mind, one after the other, word after word and you would magically fill up pages with the conversation with your Higher Self. After you read it again, you will notice the difference in the tone and the way you think than your wiser, optimistic Higher Self.

Automatic writing is not a difficult activity, and you do not need to be intuitive nor meditate on a daily basis to achieve it. Naturally, those who meditate have precedence due to their skill of silencing their mind. However, anyone can communicate with their Higher Self at will. Trust whatever you receive, even if you feel it is your imagination; we assure you, it is, in fact, true.

When Amelia first interacted with her high self, she understood the difference, due to the plethora of information presented to her. She asked a question she did not know the answer to, and yet the answers were revealed and made sense to her; they were true, loving and wise.

In time, while writing back and forth to your Higher Self, the connection will become stronger and so it will be easier to differentiate each thought. Ultimately, you will not need to write down the thoughts, but have a direct communication at any time. With practice, anyone gets better at anything. Do not get disappointed if you do not succeed direct connection during your first attempts; gradually, you will learn to clear your own thoughts, and understand infinite wisdom.

Meditation is a tool that will help you succeed in that task. Spend more time in this way clearing your thoughts, and it will become possible soon enough.

A deeper connection with your Higher Self takes you

further, awakens you, uncovers your spiritual path, and assists you in a life full of blessings. You can have a counselor at any time, just a thought away. Learn to embrace it and use it for your benefit. You have all the answers already within.

You are so powerful.

CHAPTER 60

MENTAL POWERS OF COMMUNICATION

We bring you joy from above, courage to face all doubts, will to continue living in appreciation. We connect with you through your aura with feelings, and empower your state; we talk to you through your third eye with mental images, we communicate with mental words to bring your messages. Those who are in sync with their natural powers and Higher Self can understand our communication. In this chapter we break down the direct ways of communication between physical and non-physical beings.

    We always connect from within, and those who worry or are filled with thoughts cannot acknowledge us. Remain in silence or contemplation after a prayer; sometimes we answer at once, but since you are not accustomed to silence, you do not recognize our response. Release thought and wait for our reply. You will not hear external sounds, nor see us flying with wings above your head, but you will feel we are there, see us with your mind's eye, hear us through inside words.

Some may receive all ways of communication, while others one; this is due to your own resistance and how much you allow. We will never connect with you in any way that will scare you. Some of you have a natural ability, an intuitive sense that is more awakened, so you allow more means of spiritual communication. As a kid, you had the senses cleansed and you could understand, communicate, or see through the eyes of source. As you get older, you grow distant from your natural connection and you need to readjust to our ways of communication.

One form of direct communication is through mental words in the mind, also known as- clairaudient ability. Clairaudient ability allows ideas to be communicated through a series of energetic transmissions, that are translated to the preceptor in the form of thoughts that bring new information. We provide new ideas and messages through the subconscious that are translated to the conscious as words in order to be understood. We provide the thoughts and not the words, since our natural way of communication does not include words but internal understanding. Your mind then transcribes that energy as words that your conscious mind can understand.

We form thoughts that are similar to one's own thinking for this, they can easily be overseen or ignored. These thoughts sometimes come altogether in a mass energy that we transmit through the crown chakra or come simultaneously to form ideas and sentences. If one holds resistance or a mind full of fear, worry or chatter, one does not allow us to form thoughts, and our connection gets lost. For this, it is essential to remove the chatter and find your inner peace to establish communication. To assist you with this task we have already revealed several processes in this book.

In a similar manner, clairvoyant ability is achieved. We provide ideas to the subconscious that the conscious translates them as images. Your subconscious is closely connected to your intuition that correctly translates those images to messages. Mental pictures are the same as images you see with your imagination, as we trigger the mind to connect and form patterns of pictures. Perhaps we bring you the image of a child laughing that you associate and translate as a positive sign of pleasure. The image of a monk you associate and translate as a spiritual father, and then the images connect with each other to form your understanding of our messages. In this way, we similarly bring you images in sleep state, known as "dreams".

The images are interconnected with your ability to transcribe them, so do not worry of misinterpretations. The way we provide clairvoyant messages are through your third eye that is between your eyebrows, that holds your imagination and portal of mental images. When you dream, you do not see with your eyes, but with your mental third eye that is awakened and not blocked when you are asleep.

Claircognizance is the ability to know the truth, or else described as intuition. This strong knowing is associated with inner understanding and peace accompanied by an event or action.

The fourth means of communication is the most common amongst all of you since you use it consciously or unconsciously. Clairsentience, or empathy, is the ability to feel the emotions of those around you, or sense us when we appear. Similarly, you transcribe our messages through the emotions we provide, which are always strong and caring. The feelings of unconditional love and joy are a validation we are around.

All can receive our messages, regardless if you are born with an awakened ability. Next time you pray, be aware of our answers, they may come instantly.

Can you understand them?

CHAPTER 61

REMEMBER YOUR TALENTS

We have watched you make progress as you read, uncovering the truth a chapter at a time. Now, we entrust you with a technique that is to allow your being to progress in spirit and empower your gifts. All of you are unique and hold different characteristics, because you have lived different life paths and the skills you have acquired through your lifetimes vary. All those gifts exist within, waiting to be uncovered.

While you can take any skill you choose, there are some that have already been acquired, and they are easier to use. These skills can be anything from playing the piano to languages you knew before, communicating with the spirit world, running faster, or excellence in physics and mathematics. Gifts and talents vary, and while you may have already discovered some, there are others already waiting to be revealed. These skills appear to you more easily than others, as they are skills already acquired. Some are more apparent than others, because they were used in more recent lifetimes, or they have been used in more than one life before. These skills already exist in your subconscious, and you can tune into their mastery.

Proceed without being skeptical; if you think that one activity is difficult, or believe you cannot do it because you haven't used it before, you create blockages that prevent you from remembering that skill. Sit in quiet with a piece of paper and pen in front you. Like the "automatic writing" technique we have explained in previous chapters, ask your Higher Self to reveal your skills and talents that already exist within, and can be attended to easily. Write the responses that come back through your thoughts with a clear mind, and your list will get filled with skills and activities. When you are done, read the skills and cross any of those that you hold resistance to, or that you dislike in any way. For instance if you find a skill dangerous, you are resistant, and so it will be difficult to be remembered. Start with mild skills that you find exciting and fun.

Amelia's list of past life skills and talents includes: writing, painting, weaving, leadership, even swordsmanship. Amelia has never attempted any of those skills in this lifetime, but decided to try painting. Her first painting was a successful night sky with stars. Now she can easily create beautiful art with no previous education or assistance.

It is your turn to decide upon those talents and try them. Release any expectations beforehand about how you will do. Invoke the Angels to assist you in this way.

"Please assist me to remember this skill and fully restore and accomplish its usage. Thank you, and so it is."

Remember, it is okay not to get it right the first time; it will occur slowly and with one step each time. A young child does not attempt to write first time around, even though they used that skill in many lives before. The same is with you; you will be very good at it, but that does not mean you will create a detailed painting first time around.

Be patient with yourself, and remember that you are very powerful and hold many skills already in your heart. Expansion comes in many ways and forms, but all are there to complete you.

Enjoy them.

CHAPTER 62

FULLFILLING YOUR LIFE'S PURPOSE

We are here to enlighten you so you can find your path. There is no right or wrong doing as you are free to choose your own course. Your life's purpose is waiting to be uncovered, but it is up to you to fulfill it.

With every life purpose, the world becomes better, and many souls are benefited in the process. Your life's purpose is not less than anyone else's, and it may change from lifetime to lifetime. Whether it is a book, a job you love, a lesson or an act of kindness, once it is completed, you will feel loving emotions of fulfillment, joy, appreciation, love and inner peace. You will be more in control of your thoughts and emotions, and you will feel utter joy and positivity. When you have accomplished your path, your spirituality enhances, and you no longer worry for material matters. Everyone experiences the accomplishments of a life path in different ways, yet all cherish it and have no regrets.

Your life changes for the better as you follow your Divine path; you are open to universal timing and allow your desires to flow easily to you. Whether your purpose is being a spiritual leader or a gardener, all have equal work to do and are created for a higher purpose. You see, nature has needs as well, and God sends many souls to protect and help it expand and supply.

Do you adore nature and all that it brings, or do you find pleasure in knowledge or healing? It is time to find your calling. Make a list of the things you love doing to discover your purpose. Your life's path lies in your talents and preferences. Are you creative or logical? Do you enjoy having ideas or pursuing ideas? Are you the designer or the builder of a house? Both paths are of equal importance in order to create a house; and the same is with any path; it leads to the ultimate function of the cosmos. To decide which is your path, you have to understand who you are.

Whatever your path is, it conveys joy and completion. If you feel perplexed; do not worry, ask us for help and we will reveal it to you, but remember to be aware of our signs and messages.

Whether we have brought you enlightenment, joy or guided you towards your purpose, we have completed our mission. Give yourself love, and do not be so hard on yourself. Allow some time, and all things will fall into place.

We support you.

CHAPTER 63

YOU KNOW THE ANSWER

If an idea, thought or event brings you happiness, then it resonates with your Higher Self. If it creates fear, anger or doubt then it is a warning. Many of you ask us for clarification on whether one matter is for your benefit, and whether you shall take that advice, or go to that place, or get that job. This chapter presents a simple process to assist you make your own beneficial decisions by following the clues your Higher Self sends you.

An opportunity knocks on your door, but you are hesitant. *Is this truly for my highest good? How would I know if I am to take that opportunity?* The truth is that most of the opportunities are beneficial in one way or the other. Perhaps not in the way you have wished or expect, but all of them are. If several opportunities present themselves, you must decide the best one for you; so ask and embrace the answer.

Here is an example: you have three different job opportunities, and you need to choose the most beneficial. Contemplate on all three of them for a while. What do you want to achieve? What would be your best outcome? Sometimes you ask for the most beneficial result to appear, but what if all are beneficial? No one can make that decision for you, and so you must decide and clarify within first. What is it that you seek? Flexible hours, good boss, a friendly environment, high salary or perhaps experience, things to learn? Write them all down in detail. Choose the most important first and then ask the Angels to help you decide.

Here is a prayer: *"Angels of the Light, I ask you to reveal to me the most beneficial job/result at this time that resembles these values the most. Thank you, and so it is."*

You do not need to stress over it any longer. The best outcome will appear. Beware of any possible signs that we bring. Perhaps we speak to you from within, listen to your intuition, acknowledge your feelings.

But what if you receive an offer that is not right for you? How would you know it is so? The truth is you do; you have a high knowing of whether something is good or not. What does your heart tell you? Contemplate upon your thoughts and attitude recently. Have you been positive, optimistic, happy – and then this opportunity made its way to you? Then you do not need to worry for it any longer; it is your answer. Perhaps you have been gloomy, depressed, anxious and negative; listen to your inner guidance and intuition, and follow the responses from within. Ask and be aware of the emotions; are they positive or negative? Do you want to take that opportunity, or does it make you sad, unsatisfied? We offer many processes on how to quiet your mind and listen to your inner self or intuition. If you are unsure, we are always there, and so is

THE TRUTH OF ALL THAT IS

God, and the universe. Anytime you ask, we always respond. If the opportunity is not pleasing you, ask for a better one, and believe it will arrive.

If you send negative signals to the cosmos, so it responds, as well. Were you merry or were you negative before that opportunity appeared? There is always a way to know if something is for your highest good. Step away from the crowd, be with your thoughts and ask for clarity; you will know. Your Higher Self guides you.

Listen.

CHAPTER 64

NATURE'S BLESSINGS

Take a look around in nature; this universe in which you stand is so very powerful, and beautiful that one must pause often to appreciate it. In return, nature offers blessings to those who recognize its beauty.

Blessings big and small lay all around for those who pause to appreciate. A bird sound, the rain, a sunrise, a child playing, a cat purring; you are surrounded in all moments, but do you notice them? Stop, breathe, look around; you are surrounded in love. God's beautiful work is presented before your very eyes; can you see it? What experience makes you rejoice? Perhaps the breeze on your skin, the sun light, a butterfly? You are so blessed in every moment; find the reasons why. Look around and tell us; pause to smell the flowers, enjoy the sunrise, look at the view outside your window. Observe nature to soothe your worries. Even the smallest appreciation creates a new attitude. All the beauty exists just for you in any moment.

Nature is created with so much love, and if you spend time basking in it, you receive it also. The more time you spend in nature, the more you bask in its Divine Energy. We do not ask you to plant a tree or tend your garden, but to spent time in nature, as it will shift and clear your vibration. Nature holds pure frequencies and rewards those who put their positive attention towards it. It understands who cares and who appreciates it. Nurture it, and then you shall be blessed.

One good example of nature's appreciation is with Amelia: she prayed over nature and offered much gratitude for its offerings and beauty. Her positive energies were absorbed in by Earth, and then it responded. It sent her great synchronicities, butterflies, and birds flying over her head, as if they were saying "Thank you" in return. Nothing goes unnoticed; nature may not understand words, but it knows frequency and love. Appreciate it and you will bask in its divinity, pure appreciation and high energy.

Anything that comes from nature holds high frequencies that affect your mood. For instance, standing under a tree restores and uplifts your energy; the ocean clears your negativity and brings you peace, now you even use crystals as a way of healing. There are many more examples and benefits that are nature's gifts to you.

Your daily life is filled with moments of magnificence and it only takes a second to notice. Nature is all around; find its blessings and you will be rewarded.

Nature exists just for you.

CHAPTER 65

WE CARRY THE PAIN AWAY

When you are in pain, we hear your prayers; when you are in distress, we know. We feel when you are out of balance, and we want to soothe you with loving emotions. We bring you this chapter for those times when you feel alone, lost and worried, to nurture you like the mother does to her crying child. Whenever you are unwell, read the lines of this chapter to bring you higher levels of frequency, and restore your pain back to Light.

This is for those who are hurting, feel our words as an embrace around your shoulders, like a hug from your friends, as we are here and you are never alone. You may feel gloomy or lost, you may have lost someone dear to you or feel negative emotions. No matter the reason of your grief and sadness, it hides a blessing; it lets you know what you are missing so it will be restored. If you lost a person dear, you grieve for that missing part, you recognize the gap and yearn to complete it. None who leave their physical bodies cease to be. You are to meet them again. Their passing brings you carriage and there are lessons to be taught. It marks a new area of change.

When you grieve you feel incomplete and yearn for fulfillment; you are lost and what to be found, you cry for help as you want to be saved. Your tears are not lost; we feel you grieving; we know you are hurting, we watch you struggle. Feel comforted by knowing we are next to you. Allow us to soothe your pain; let us assist you to happiness. Ask us to step in and ease your pain with these words: *"Angels of comfort I ask that you soothe my hurting and restore the missing piece from my life so that I feel whole and happy. Carry away the grief, ease my pain. And so it is."*

Allow our Divine assistance to run through your body and merge our vibrations with your own, to restore you to well-being. Feel our presence surround you and bask in the warmth of Divine Light. Your prayers have been heard, the struggle ends; we bring you joy. Allow grief to step away and be replaced; do not focus on your misery, but the change that is ahead. You are evolving, and this is a part of a Divine plan even if you cannot see it. You are part of this plan, and the sooner you find your way, the sooner you will be a part of it. Acknowledge the pain, grieve and then allow the pieces to fall into place, and lead you to your next great path. Trust that all is taken care of, and you will be whole again, as that is the natural state that you are created to be: complete and happy.

Let the pain wash away; there are great things up ahead. No matter your journey so far, no matter the pain now, you have survived, you are alive, and your path does not end here. You are alright, and you have great things to accomplish.

We bring you to the Light.

CHAPTER 66

BE A LEADER

Allow the experiences to lead you to where you are supposed to go. There is no reaching your destination, not completing your path if you are walking towards the opposite direction. We have mentioned several times already that whatever comes is not random. There is a bigger plan for all and if you could embrace what comes in your way, you shall thrive. Do not think too much; life is simpler if you trust all will work out alright. A leader is someone who lights the way so others follow. You can be that leader, and light up the darkness in times of need.

Perhaps you received bad news, or a new illness has spread toward the Atlantic; perhaps a relative passed away, or you are struggling with debt. We know these events are far from pleasant, but do you add to their negative flow, or do you allow these events to pass by? Resistance is never a positive experience, but it adds more negativity in your life. Whenever you receive negative news, let them go and wash away the way a tornado passes and leaves, the way the waves of the sea wash away the waste. Acknowledge the news, yet do not resist; they have come to bring a message, a warning, a lesson, to force you towards the opposite end of the string. If you heard of death, celebrate your life; if you heard of an illness, appreciate your health; receive the will of well-being instead of adding to the pain; and so, you become stronger. Let the negative events wash away leaving you intact and strong, while others enter the tornado come out scarred and hurt. Detach yourself from any negative news or experiences; deny their effect, be shielded from their hardships and so they will not have an affect on you.

Ask us for assistance, so negative events do not effect you, and we will bring you strength.

"Angels of the Light, surround me in this hour of need and protect me so that I am not affected by hardships and sadness from this event that occurred. Shield me so I do not experience this pain; be with me until it washes away. And so it is."

We shall bring you courage and strength; have no fear, for you are surrounded by love. Do not add to the pain, do not resist it as you cannot change what has already taken place, but let it pass you by, unaffected. You can only change your responses towards it. Do not consider yourself insensible, but courageous. The weak need the stronger to help them deal with the pain, to follow their lead and be stronger. The world needs leaders and followers to raise others up; be that leader. Do not get affected by hardships, but break through, wiser. The world needs you to show them the way. Be shielded and move forth with joy and purpose; you have much to give, yet none will suffice if you are sad or fearful.

Be the change the world wants to see. There are lessons to come, be prepared to face them with courage and let them bring you knowledge and wisdom. Stay strong;

                        the world needs leaders like you.

CHAPTER 67

FIND YOUR TRUTH

Most of you cannot see us, and for that you doubt our existence. But we are not here to convince anyone of what is true, nor save those that do not want to be saved. We reach out to those who seek answers and those who are ready to change their lives and find their inner purpose. We do not ask that you believe our words, but find your truth within.

Contemplate upon these questions: *Who am I and why did I come on Earth? Who is God, has He created the Angels and all other beings as well as me? Do I believe I am pure positive energy and have good means? Do I believe I have come to enjoy and love and expand? Am I only a physical body?*

Your connection with the non-physical assures you of the answers. Do you feel the confirmation from within, the emotions that arise from you? You hold the answers already; you do not need convincing. You are reading this book because your Higher Self wants you to remember who you are. Take a moment and consider those questions; search inside yourself to find the answers. If you are true to yourself and connected to your divinity, follow your intuition; you will find the answers that you seek. We do not teach you new things, but remind you what you lost, who you are and what you came here to achieve.

How many of our teachings resonate with you? Release the old beliefs and embrace the new. As you read our words, did they have a positive impact? Did they bring up fear and sadness? If you read with an open heart, you will know the answers to all those questions.

We are here to guide you, and whether you believe us or not, we still love all of you. Accept our guidance or not, believe our teachings or create your own, either way live in joy and love, and see the beauty of the world. This is your main goal in all lifetimes. Even if you have different beliefs, make this one the same: Live in joy and love.

This book is only the start, and many more shall follow. If you judge and deny the words we bring, it is all right, in another lifetime you will come to realize the world of God and move further in your expansion. There is no end and there is no right now. There is nothing that we ask you to do if you won't follow our words willingly. The time shall come that we will meet in the Light. The rest of you physical beings, now reawakened to the truth, we welcome you and bring you many blessings. You will not be the same; you have expanded in being, and you shall rise greater than ever. There are many more things to do and experience, but the best is yet to come, in any lifetime that you are, and in any lifetime that you are going. You are enlightened, you are new. We welcome you in the Light. Nothing shall be the same again.

You are evolving.

CHAPTER 68

DISCOVER YOUR POTENTIAL

Loving yourself is a crucial step to create your life. Respect and love your being as you are, recognize your exceptional power, love what you do. The place you stand now is a starting point to glorious experiences that follow. Spend time working on your skills, attending to your thoughts, admiring who you are and who you are becoming. Remember to shield yourself as you are becoming more powerful and more sensitive to anything negative. You are so much more than you give yourself, credit for.

You were created from positive energy when God wanted to form the most beautiful beings; out of that attention, you sufficed. You are those beings, and we want you to really see it as well. See beyond your imperfections and fears; you are so capable and powerful – if you could only know how much you can achieve, you would not bother looking for completion outside of yourself. Everything begins from you, and we urge you to discover all your potential now. Humanity only knows a limited percent of everything they are and can achieve. If you only let go of fear, doubt and reasoning, you will see with the eyes of source, feel with pure positive emotions, bask in love and appreciation.

To uncover the rest of who you really are, love all that you are. Be all that you came here to be.

You are worthy.

CHAPTER 69

SIGNS OF AN AWAKENED SPIRIT

If you attend to your thoughts and energies with devotion and positive attention, your life shifts and enhances. You receive more Light or positive energy and are more aware of our guidance. In this way, your life takes a rapid shift towards improvement and the things you want are more accessible to you. The paradigm we want you to follow is finding beauty in every corner so you shift blockages, fear and hate from your experience. The changes you attain once you awaken are advantageous. Did we succeed our mission to awaken you?

Once you awaken, you will shift towards the fifth dimension that will bring certain changes in your experience. The rapid changes that you experience firstly come through your thoughts. If you enhance your reality with positive attitude, your life takes a shift towards beautiful experiences. The more you focus, the more you shift, the more you shift, the more beauty surrounds your and you enjoy life more. You live in the moment, live with all your heart and enjoy everything and everyone that interacts with you. You are uplifted as more energy radiates within you. You invite well-being into your experience and your physical body is more attune to you. You feel good in your own skin, beautiful, healthy and your mood is mostly uplifted.

Once you awaken, you interact with people and experiences that are positive and matter to you. People that do not share your optimism or values are not a part of your life any further. For this, many people that you had a close bond with, may no longer be as close to you.

Generally, your life transforms with anything that adds to your expansion and happiness, and becomes detoxified from people, events and circumstances that do not match your high frequency. If at any time you find yourself in an unlikely environment, it will drain your energy more than usual if given attention; but do not worry, as discussed you can easily shift your attention so it has no effect.

Moreover, when you awaken, you are guided towards beautiful experiences and towards your life's path more freely. You enjoy more of the things you desire and find it easier to accomplish certain matters that were otherwise seen as tasks.

Your path is easier to attend to, as you follow the guidance of your Spirit Guides through your enhanced intuition. Your Higher Self can direct you easily towards goals, so blockages are removed from your way. You know whether something is right or not; and so, you move towards a positive direction in your life; you no longer feel stuck, you find your purpose and rhythm. Signs are revealed to you as we and the cosmos communicate with you often, and you can translate our messages. You find yourself in the perfect moment, the perfect time, as synchronicities become a part of your daily life. You recognize these signs and know them as such. Angels, Spirit Guides and many other loving beings surround you and wish to assist you, and your high energies allow us to do it. Notice our signs to you.

You lose sense of time. You do not notice it, as it is no longer a part of your existence. You belong in higher realms where time does not keep you grounded, but moves you gracefully. It otherwise feels as if you have so much fun that you do not see the clock ticking; you do not feel time pass you by. Time is no longer a burden; you flow with your own timing.

Those awakened have a different shine that others recognize. People give you compliments often, as you radiate joy and energy. Others are uplifted around you, and you share your energy with anyone that is in need of it. You become selfless as you move further away from your third dimensional ego self; you share joy and love with others. Assisting them brings you uplifting energy and a sense of power and delight.

You become wiser. You acquire a deeper knowing that connects you with All-that-Is. You understand your path and experiences, you no longer feel lost or misunderstood; you find reassurance and completion from within. You do not turn to others for uplifting energy; you do not care of what others think, for you really see and understand things your way. You do not bother persuading others, but respect their free will and appreciate their difference.

If you recognize all or some of these sings, then you have now succeeded; you have awakened, and moved to the fifth dimension, as well as accomplished self-knowledge. You understand the basic values and experiences of the world; you are now ready to rejoice life. You know your power, as well as find joy and completion within. We mentioned only some of the signs you will experience, since the ways vary for everyone. Whatever those signs are, bask in your glory; you are capable, you are powerful; you *do* belong in a deeper world full of expansion, and you are expanding yourself.

You are now awakened.

CHAPTER 70

YOUR AWAKENING

The knowledge and exercises of this book hold power not only to the teachings and truths revealed but to the energy as well. As you release wrong ideals, replace them with new values and live as we described you will succeed exceptional growth in body and spirit, in experiences and relationships and towards spiritual awakening.

The closer you are to your life's path, the closer you live according to the will of God, and the more you feel complete, eager, loved and bask in the abundance of the world. Part of your spiritual awakening is to restore your beliefs, and give meaning in all that you do. By awakening to All-that-Is, you take control of your own emotions and create a satisfying life; you evolve in spirit; you find your life's purpose. This book was created to offer you the road back to fulfillment, love, success, ease and fun.

Years ago, people were not ready for this book; if it was

written earlier, it would have been dismissed and judged. People now are ready to embrace it, and follow its teachings because they are more awakened to the truth. It is the will of God that souls who reincarnate come about with more knowledge and with more of their Divine gifts, to embrace existence and find their path effortlessly. The more humanity expands, the more people are reawakened to the truth and find their own purpose. The more of you succeed and fulfill your life's path, the more positive energies you uncover for others to use and awaken themselves. You are all ready to know these words, and so you were chosen to read them. We have guided you here to find your path to well-being. Spiritual awakening is understanding the universal flow, being more connected to you divinity, appreciating physical experiences yet thrive in spirit.

Remember: you all came here for a reason and that is to complete your life's path and enjoy life, spread love and receive love. You are ready to succeed. Be more aware in the following days as we bring you signs. You will know our messages that will lead you towards your life's path. Do not be afraid if you feel stuck or disoriented; relax, breathe and remind yourself that all is alright. You are where you supposed to be. There is nothing moving against your path now. Do not resist happiness; choose your thoughts carefully and be aware of what you create. Make the best of it.

We watch you, assist you, love you. We are your true siblings. Brothers and sisters, enjoy your life and remember even the slightest downfall can be a blessing in disguise. You are alright.

We love you and surround you, always.

CHAPTER 71

MESSAGE FROM GOD

I am All-that-Is. I encourage you to embrace anything that comes in your path; they are given to you for a reason; embrace them and live in prosperity and love. I am here now to uplift your spirits and bring this book into completion. It has achieved its purpose and has offered you the knowledge that was needed to move you forth into your life enlightened. I speak directly to all of you, and gather your focused attention for several moments to open the Gates of Heaven and offer you a glimpse of My love.

Thoughts and ideas that run through your mind every second are welcomed if they are pure and uplifting. Those are thoughts and emotions that offer you happiness and joy, resonate with your being and make your energies expand. The more you expand in this way, the more you open the "Doors of Heaven" to receive pure and positive experiences. When I say "Heaven," I do not mean a place, for such a place only exists in imagination. Heaven is every positive thought; anything uplifting, anything wonderful. Heaven is unconditional love; Heaven is getting closer to who you truly are, your divinity, closer to the Angels, closer to Me. Bring Heaven into your life by focusing only on what pleases you. You were created out of pure positive energy, and so you are, and it is my Will that you continue to be.

I do see all of you who struggle and are filled with negativity and low vibrations, those who attract unfortunate events and fear. I send my hand to those, as well, and to all of you, for you are from the same loving energy. I offer you assistance to uplift and bring you back to all that you can be. You are unlimited, Divine, powerful and pure. I assist all and embrace all who call upon us. I am within all of you and show you the way.

Be open, be receptive. Assist others who are in need, as in this way, you assist yourself also; all together we are one, we are complete. We all are energy and power, and we are all the same.

Be uplifted, give uplifting energy, spread love and joy, and be all that you were created to be. There are no limitations; all of you are different yet all the same. Fear not; I am with you. I am assisting you, I am there to catch you if you fall, help you if you call. I am around always and forever, alongside all of you.

You have unlimited potential and power. It is my will that you fulfill your path and enjoy every lifetime as you are supposed to. Learn and expand, live and love, for you always live, never endingly, only in different layers, different places, different ages and different galaxies. Merely, you are always near me, for I am never away; I reside in your heart. Every time you are in need call and I shall appear. I will uplift you, I will expand you. Let me show you how much you can do, how much you can achieve. Keep Me close to your heart and together we will bring miracles.

    I am Yourself, your Brother, your Angel, your Creator, your World. I am All-that-Is, and you are too.

PRAYERS AND ANGEL INVOCATIONS

To declare your appreciation:
"Thank you for all those moments that I felt pure and happy; thank you for this moment right now that I am alive and radiate energy. I recognize that I create my own reality, and I am to use that for good, for myself and for all."
(From Chapter 7 - You create your own world)

To release old beliefs:
"I accept who I was. I am thankful for all those things, people and events that were in my path up until today, because they helped be who I am now. I release, and let go of the old, so the new can make its way to me, with better experiences that only bring loving emotions. I am ready to welcome it now. I say goodbye to the old and hello to the new. And so it is."
(From Chapter 33 – Life review)

To realize your power:
"I am an unlimited being of creation and I create my everyday experiences. I now acknowledge this power that I hold, and choose to shift it towards joy, love and appreciation. The desires I want are ready to enter my experience. I

accept why they haven't made their way towards me yet, and I now, consciously remove these limiting beliefs that kept me from those desires. I choose to live a life full of beautiful experiences, financial and spiritual abundance, abundance of loving interactions, of health and wellness, and of the truth of who I really I am. I am capable, I am worthy of those new experiences, and I now allow them to enter into my being and into my life. I do not contradict them any longer. I am eager, loved, worthy. I am abundant. I create my own experience and I choose to fill them with joy, love and all those material and spiritual things I seek. I am now ready for a new beginning, a new life experience. I let go, I allow. And so it is."

(From Chapter 36 – Welcome your life experience)

To remove limiting beliefs:

"Angels of the Light, I ask you to come forth right now and help me clear up those false beliefs and replace them with new ones that do not contradict my perfect state of being into the area of health. Thank you, and so it is."

(From the exercise Chapter 38 – Remove blockages)

To summon forth the energy of your desires:

"I am now ready to receive the flow of abundance for this certain desire to now enter my life. I lay in acknowledgment that you will move circumstances and events to bring it to me when the time is right. I lovingly ask you Energy, to assist this event to enter my life experience easily and effortlessly. Allow the cosmos to bring it to me as described, or bring me something better. I dearly thank you. It is for my best well-being and for the greatest and highest good of all."

(From the exercise Chapter 44 – Achieve an abundant mindset)

To believe in your power:
"Angels of the Light, I call upon you now to bring my awareness on such item or matter, to help me really see, really believe. I am ready to awaken. Open my eyes to the truth. And so it is."

(From Chapter 53 – Ask for a sign)

To shield yourself:
"My powerful shining Light, I ask that you are protected by unwelcomed negative energies of others. Shield and rest your power with the help of several Lighted Angels. Merge your shine with mine, save me from any darkness and negativity. And so it is."

(From Chapter 57 – Shield yourself)

For clarity:
"Angels of the Light, I ask you to reveal to me the most beneficial job/result at this time that resembles these values the most. Thank you, and so it is."

(From Chapter 63 – You know the answer)

To soothe your pain:
"Angels of comfort I ask that you soothe my hurting and restore the missing piece from my life so that I feel whole and happy. Carry away the grief, ease my pain. And so it is."

(From Chapter 65 – We carry the pain away)

For protection:
"Angels of the Light, surround me in this hour of need and protect me so that I am not affected by hardships and sadness from this event that occurred. Shield me so I do not experience this pain; be with me until it washes away. And so it is."

(From Chapter 66 – Be a leader)

NOTE FROM THE AUTHOR:

Did you enjoy this book? If so, will you help the Angel's journey "Awaken" more people? Leave your amazing review on: http://www.amazon.com/ It would really matter to me.

If someone you care about is a believer, send him or her a copy of this book. Help them on their journey to spiritual transformation.
Sign up to my exclusive newsletter and get an instant 20% discount. Also have access to free bonus materials, read enlightening articles, receive updates on future projects.
You can sign up here: http://ameliabert.com/
And follow me on social media:

https://www.facebook.com/theangelbook/
https://twitter.com/Author_AmeliaB
https://www.linkedin.com/in/ameliabert

As a **gift** to you that you have made it his far, I give you a free Angel meditation for wealth. In this meditation I channel the words of the Angels in the recording, and you get to have It for free!
Go to http://bit.ly/24qLSRq add it to your cart, and then on check out add this coupon code: ***Freegift44***
You will receive it via email in the next few hours!
Many blessings to you.

Amelia

GET YOUR ANSWERS FROM THE ANGELS DIRECTLY:

Do you want to connect with Amelia and the Angels to get direct assistance on your path, and answers to your questions?
Amelia is currently offering intuitive readings with your Guardian Angels and Spirit Guides. All you have to do is reach out.
We help you with an exclusive one time discount of 20% for any intuitive readings in the website:
http://bit.ly/1LGvTTT

Your answers are only a few clicks away.

OWN UNIQUE HIGH ENERGY ARTWORK

Hurry to get the original painting pieces of Amelia Bert. Those spiritual paintings were created with Angel inspiration and contain high energy that empower the space and people of their environment.

There are limited paintings, original and signed by Amelia Bert. Order and get your with free shipping worldwide!

http://bit.ly/1T7N3lz

ABOUT THE AUTHOR:

Amelia Bert is a freelance author and online journalist. At twenty five, she discovered her intuitive side, and mastered the clairaudient and clairvoyant ability to connect with spirit. She chooses to solely communicate with lighted spirits such as Angels that guide and inspire her.

Her book "The Truth of All that Is" was created as a result of her spiritual growth and ability to communicate with the angels. After months of meditation and spiritual connection they guided her to write that book. Working closely with the Angels, she gathers wisdom and information to share with the world. Through her books, she aims to help others make a connection with their higher consciousness and discover their life's purpose.

Amelia has a degree in English language and literature. She spends her time time writing, learning from the Angels, and painting. She lives with her fiance and three cats and wants to travel the world.

She wants to hear from you! Don't be shy, connect with her here: amelia@ameliabert.com

Printed in Great Britain
by Amazon